ABT BOX®

grades
2-3

Arts and Crafts

THE BEST OF
THE MAILBOX®
MAGAZINE

The best arts-and-crafts activities from
the 1998–2004 issues of *The Mailbox*® magazine

* **Easy Art Tips**

* **Fall Activities**

* **Winter Activities**

* **Spring Activities**

* **Anytime Activities**

* **Timesaving Index**

Managing Editor: Kelly Robertson

Editorial Team: Becky S. Andrews, Kimberley Bruck, Sharon Murphy, Debra Liverman, Diane Badden, Thad H. McLaurin, Karen A. Brudnak, Juli Docimo Blair, Hope Rodgers, Dorothy C. McKinney

Production Team: Lori Z. Henry, Pam Crane, Rebecca Saunders, Chris Curry, Sarah Foreman, Theresa Lewis Goode, Greg D. Rieves, Eliseo De Jesus Santos II, Barry Slate, Donna K. Teal, Zane Williard, Tazmen Carlisle, Kathy Coop, Marsha Heim, Lynette Dickerson, Mark Rainey, Amy Kirtley-Hill

www.themailbox.com

Table of Contents

Easy Art Tips

Individual Paint Palettes

Take the pain out of class painting projects with individual paint palettes! Give each child a five-inch square of leftover laminating film. To disperse paint, squeeze dollops of desired tempera paints directly on the palettes. When it's time for cleanup, allow the paint on the palettes to dry before removing it (it crumbles easily). Presto! The palettes are ready to be reused!

Charlotte Cross
Fletcher Elementary, Fletcher, OK

Awesome Art Mats

These awesome art mats make cleanup as easy as one, two, three! Have each student personalize and decorate an 18" x 24" sheet of construction paper. Laminate the paper mats and store them in an accessible area. Before your next art activity, pass out the mats and have students place them on top of their desks. When it is time for cleanup, simply wipe the mats with a damp paper towel or rinse them in the sink. What an easy way to keep desks clean!

Melinda Casida, Crowly Elementary, Visalia, CA

Handy Handles

Get a handle on messy sponge painting! Hot-glue an empty glue stick container to the back of each sponge shape. Students grip the glue stick handles instead of the sponges. And that means paint-covered fingers are a thing of the past!

Janet Truitt, Hayes Grade Center, Ada, OK

Lost Marker Caps

If your students frequently lose the caps to their markers, try this tip! Whenever you get ready to discard markers that have dried up or are no longer usable, place their caps in a special container in your classroom. When a student loses a marker's cap, he simply goes to the container to find a replacement.

Jacqueline Margraf, Wading River School
Wading River, NY

Glue Refills

Take this approach, and students always have glue when they need it! Near your sink or supply area, post a sign that says, "Filling Station." Then confirm that each child's glue bottle is personalized. When a student is almost out of glue, she drops off her glue bottle at the filling station before she leaves for the day. Each afternoon, refill (and return) glue bottles as needed.

Sandy Preston
North Street Elementary School
Brockway, PA

Portable Paint Holders

Don't throw away those cardboard drink holders—use them for paint projects! Set clean, empty yogurt containers in a cardboard drink holder. Add water to one container for cleaning paintbrushes, and pour different colors of paint into the remaining containers. If time runs out before students complete their artwork, cover the entire holder with foil for overnight storage. No more spills!

Sharon Fien
Parkdale Elementary
East Aurora, NY

Sunny Pencil Boxes

Spread some back-to-school sunshine and minimize messy desks with these eye-catching pencil holders!

Materials for one pencil box:

bottom 2½" of a cereal box

strips of green poster board, 2½" wide (to cover the sides of the precut box)

one 7" yellow construction paper semicircle

one 2½" x 6" strip of yellow construction paper

one 1½" x 5" strip of colorful construction paper

construction paper scraps

crayons or markers

glue

scissors

Steps:

1. Glue the green poster board strips to the four sides of the precut cereal box.
2. Cut out facial features from the construction paper scraps and glue them to the semicircle to make a cute sun character.
3. Glue the sun inside the back panel of the holder.
4. Cut the strip of yellow paper into short lengths. Glue the resulting sun rays around the edge of the sun.
5. Personalize the remaining construction paper strip and glue it to the front panel of the holder.

Elizabeth Searls Almy
Greensboro, NC

Schoolwork Frame-Ups

Make these fabulous frame-ups at the beginning of the school year to display students' work all year. Glue the ends of four poster board strips (two 2" x 12" strips and two 2" x 14" strips) together to create a rectangle. When the resulting frame is dry, decorate it as desired. Next turn the frame over and center a gallon-size resealable plastic bag over the project. Securely tape the bottom and sides of the bag to the frame. Then open the bag, carefully insert the end of a stapler, and staple the bag (just below the zipper) to the frame. Finally, press lengths of half-inch self-adhesive magnetic tape around the perimeter of the back of the project. A student slips a work sample into his frame and then proudly displays his project on his family's refrigerator. Encourage students to replace their work samples often!

Elizabeth Searls Almy

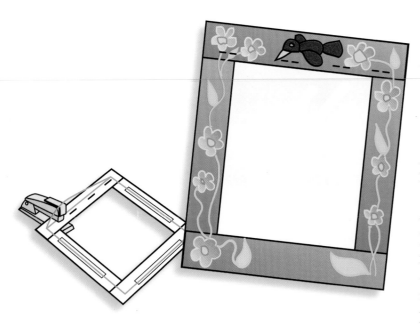

Sunflower Patch

To begin, dip a damp sponge piece into a shallow container of brown paint. Repeatedly press the sponge (reloading it as needed) onto a 12" x 18" sheet of white art paper to make four large, evenly spaced sunflower centers. Allow the paint to dry; then use yellow paint and a second piece of sponge to paint the remainder of the paper. When dry, cut a sun shape around each sunflower center. Glue a 1" x 12" green paper stem to the back of each flower and then arrange the sunflowers on a 9" x 12" sheet of blue paper. Glue each stem and flower to the paper. Trim off overhanging stems and display the sunny flowers for all to see!

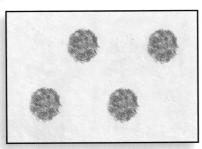

Sunny Flowers

Cultivate a crop of cheery sunflower blooms! To prepare, cut a few kitchen sponges into approximately 1" x 3" pieces and make several four-inch circle templates for students to share. Pour yellow tempera paint into a shallow container. Also set out paintbrushes and brown and green tempera paint. To make a painting, trace a circle on the upper half of a vertically positioned 12" x 18" sheet of paper. Fill the circle with brown-paint fingerprints to resemble a flower center. Dip a prepared sponge into the yellow paint and then press it onto the paper to make a petal. Continue making petals around the flower center, reloading the paint as necessary. Then paint a green stem and leaves.

Jenna Lea Ott, Mary Jo Burkell, Anne Marie Hallinan, and Helen Kelley
Mother Seton School
Emmitsburg, MD

Designer Desktags

These student-designed desktags are sure to earn rave reviews during open house! For the base, make three lengthwise accordion folds in a 6" x 18" strip of construction paper. Unfold the paper, squeeze a trail of glue along the center crease, and fold the paper in half. Then display the paper with the fold at the top as shown. Next, trace letter stencils or cutouts onto colorful construction paper to personalize the desktag. Decorate and cut out the letters and then glue them to the base. Trim the ends of the base as desired.

Pam Temerowski
Green Acres Elementary
Warren, MI

Apple Notecards

Whether students use these notecards for open house invitations or to tell their families about a great school week, they'll be a bushel of fun to prepare and deliver! To make one notecard, write a desired message on the lined side of a 4" x 6" index card. Set it aside. Use a pattern at the top of page 82 to make a red apple cutout. Then cut the apple into narrow vertical strips and set the strips in order on a work surface.

Next, glue the strips in order on the blank side of the index card, leaving a narrow space between them. Color a stem; then make a construction paper leaf and glue it in place. Complete the illustrated side of the index card with a title or the name of the intended recipient(s). After the glue dries, this one-of-a-kind notecard will be ready for hand delivery!

"Apple-tizing" Prints

Students can use this fun printing technique to decorate a bushel of school-related items such as folders, nametags, notebooks, and more! Pour red and green tempera paints into individual shallow containers. Place the item to be decorated on a flat, newspaper-covered surface. To make an apple print, dip one end of a large marshmallow into the red paint and then press it onto the item. To make a leaf, insert a toothpick into one end of a small marshmallow (for a handle) and then dip the small marshmallow into the green paint and press it near the top of an apple print. When the paint is dry, use a black permanent marker to draw stems.

Elizabeth Searls Almy
Greensboro, NC

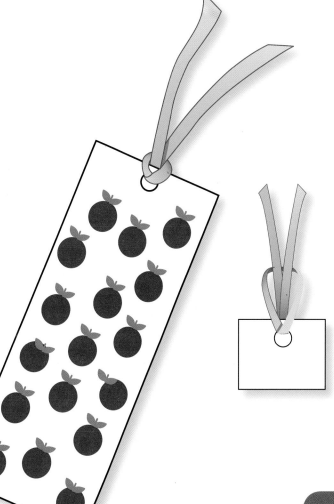

Back-to-School Bookmark

This decorative bookmark is sure to promote a bushel of reading! To make a bookmark, use red paint to make a number of thumbprints on a 2" x 6" piece of white tagboard. Allow the paint to dry. Then, with the project vertically positioned, use a marker to add leaves and stems to the prints so that they resemble apples. Hole-punch the top of the project. Next, fold a 12-inch length of ribbon in half. Push the folded end through the hole, poke the ribbon ends through the resulting loop, and then gently pull the ends snug to make a tassel.

Fancy Apples

These apples are unique and that's no yarn! Begin with a tagboard apple cutout (pattern at the bottom of page 82). Working atop a paper towel, cover the apple with a thin layer of glue. Next, lay individual four-inch strips of red yarn horizontally across the apple. Keep the yarn lengths close together and let the ends extend beyond the edges of the cutout. Continue until the apple is completely covered with yarn. When the project is dry, trim away excess yarn. Glue a green felt leaf and a brown felt stem to the project, and it's ready to adorn a class tree.

Rebecca Racciato
Five Points Elementary School
Bangor, PA

Autumn's Apples

When it's apple-pickin' time, pick this project! Prepare a half-apple template similar to the one shown. Trace the template onto folded construction paper six times, each time aligning the straight edge of the template with the fold. Cut out the tracings. Also cut a stem and a leaf from construction paper.

To assemble the apple, spread glue on the top surface of a folded cutout. Align a second folded cutout atop the glue and then spread glue on the top surface of this cutout. Repeat the process with each cutout. On top of the final cutout, lay the stem near the fold. Then pick up the project and press the top and bottom surfaces together. Next, lay the project on its side. Working around the apple, place a drop of white tempera paint in the crease of every (or every other) apple section, fold the section closed, and rub the paper to spread the paint. Add the leaf and the apple is ready to display!

Darcy Brown
Ward Elementary
Winston-Salem, NC

"Thumb" Apples!

These apple trees are truly "thumb-thing" special! To begin, tear a tree trunk shape from brown paper and glue it on a 9" x 12" sheet of white construction paper. Use green tempera paint and a sponge to paint the tree's foliage. When the green paint is dry, pour a mixture of liquid soap and red tempera paint into a shallow pan. Use the paint to make a desired number of red thumb-print apples on and near the tree. Allow drying time. Then use crayons or markers to add colorful details and a background scene.

adapted from an idea by
Jane Manuel
Wellington, TX

Colorful Autumn Leaves

Bring the beauty of fall indoors with this two-day project! On the first day, make three colorful collages. To do this, cut patches of red, yellow, and orange from magazines. Sort the pieces by color. Glue each resulting collection onto a 6" x 9" rectangle of like-colored construction paper, until the paper is completely covered.

On the second day, draw and color a well-branched tree on a 12" x 18" sheet of light blue construction paper. Then repeatedly trace a leaf template on the back of each collage. Cut out the leaves and glue them on (or near) the tree so that their bright fall colors show!

Dawn Hanson
Cornerstone Christian School
Olympia, WA

Fabulous Fall Foliage

To prepare, partially fill each of several shallow containers with a different fall color of tempera paint. Place a clean bottle brush in each container. To begin, tear a tree trunk shape from a 4" x 9" rectangle of brown paper and glue it on a 9" x 12" sheet of construction paper. Then use the paints and brushes to create colorful fall foliage. When the paint is dry, add crayon and marker details to complete the scene.

Catherine Della Torre
Woodside School
River Vale, NJ

Pretty As a Picture

It's easy for students to try their hand at the art technique called *pointillism* by making these fall trees. To begin, cut a tree trunk that has plenty of branches from brown construction paper. Glue the cutout to a sheet of paper. Dip a pencil eraser or cotton swab in one color of tempera paint; then press it repeatedly onto the area on and above the tree branches. Similarly dip another pencil eraser (or cotton swab) in a second color of paint, and press it repeatedly in the same general area. Continue in this manner, using a variety of colors until colorful dots cover the tree branches and the area that surrounds them. Also paint a few stray dots near the base of the tree to represent fallen leaves. When the paint has dried, mount the project on a slightly larger sheet of colorful construction paper. Be sure to have the students admire their paintings from afar; then, as a class, discuss how the dots merge together to create trees that are full of color!

Amy Erickson
Montello School
Lewiston, ME

Lovely Leaves

To make a leaf, drizzle liquid tempera paints in a variety of fall colors onto a 9" x 12" sheet of white construction paper. Then, using the teeth of a plastic comb, swirl the paint colors together until a desired effect is achieved. When the paint is dry, cut a large leaf shape from the project. Mount the cutout onto a slightly larger piece of fall-colored construction paper; then trim the construction paper to create an eye-catching border.

Brightening the Breezes

With their dangling legs dancing in the breezes, these leaf people are certain to stir up the feeling of fall. To begin, make one large leaf cutout using the pattern on page 83. Then make four smaller leaf cutouts using the patterns on page 84. Use markers to draw a face on the larger leaf. Glue four accordion-folded construction paper strips to the back of the larger leaf for arms and legs. To finish your leaf person, glue the remaining leaves to the dangling ends of the strips.

Carolyn Williams
North Augusta Elementary
North Augusta, SC

"Hand-some" Leaves

When it comes to making these lovely leaves, students will be more than happy to lend a hand! To make a hand-print leaf, paint the palm side of a hand using fall-colored tempera paint (orange, yellow, red, brown). Press the hand, with fingers spread, onto a sheet of white paper. When the painted paper has dried, draw a jagged outline around the handprint with a fall-colored crayon and then color the white areas inside the outline with a different fall-colored crayon. Cut out the leaf, and the fall foliage is ready to display!

Sharon Hackley
Kingman, AZ

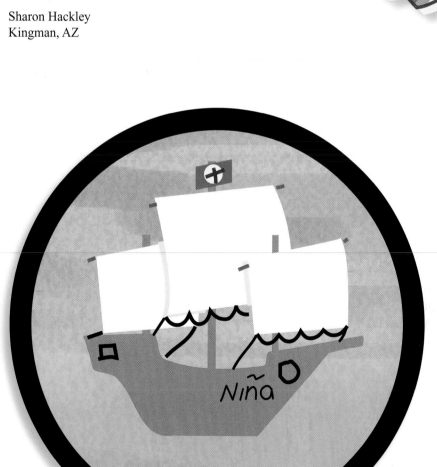

Sail On!

Look what's on the horizon—a seaworthy project for Columbus Day! Cut an eight-inch circle from white construction paper. Using watercolors, paint ocean waters on the bottom half of the circle and a colorful sky on the top half. While this dries, cut out a ship's hull, sails, and masts from construction paper scraps. Add details to the cutouts with crayons or markers. To assemble the project, glue the painted circle atop a slightly larger, black construction paper circle; then glue the construction paper cutouts to the painted surface. Land ahoy!

Squirrel Sighting

In a nutshell, these bushy-tailed critters are simply too cute to pass up!

Materials for one project:
4" x 12" piece of gray construction paper
2" x 4" piece of gray construction paper
4" x 8" piece of gray construction paper
4" square of gray construction paper
construction paper scraps
4" leaf template
six 4" squares of construction paper in fall colors
glue
scissors
crayons

Steps:

1. **To make the body,** roll the 4" x 12" piece of gray paper into a cylinder and glue the overlapping edges together. Set it aside to dry.

2. **For the head,** trim the four-inch square of gray paper into a desired shape and decorate it. Keeping the seam at the back of the cylinder, glue the head to the front of the body.

3. **For the tail,** trim the 4" x 8" piece of gray paper into a desired shape. If desired, gently curl the tail before gluing it to the back of the body.

4. **For the feet,** fold in half the 2" x 4" piece of gray paper and cut out two matching feet. Add desired details and glue the feet to the body.

5. **For the bed of leaves,** trace the leaf template onto the remaining construction paper squares. Cut out the leaves. Arrange them as desired and glue the overlapping surfaces. Glue the squirrel atop the leaves.

Rita Arnold
Alden Hebron Grade School
Hebron, IL

Night Owls

Position a sheet of drawing paper vertically. Use dark heavy strokes to color a tree trunk along the left or right edge of the paper. Also color a tree limb that extends across the bottom of the page. Then paint the entire paper with black watercolor paint. When the paint is dry, round the corners of a 3" x 5" and a 2" x 3" brown construction paper rectangle. Add crayon or marker details to each cutout to resemble the body of an owl. Glue the cutouts just above the tree limb. Glue a large pretzel at the top of the large cutout and a small pretzel at the top of the small cutout. When the glue dries, use tempera paint to add a beak, eyes, and feet as shown. Press a black paper pupil in each eye before the paint dries.

Freda McKittrick
Troy Grade School
Troy, KS

Pretty Patterned Pumpkin

These pretty pumpkins will be the pick of the patch! Sketch a large pumpkin shape on a 12" x 18" sheet of orange construction paper and then cut out the shape. From a different color of paper, cut out strips, circles, and other desired shapes. (Provide a hole puncher and/or assorted templates as desired.) Arrange the pieces on the pumpkin in a pleasing pattern and glue them in place. Add a green paper stem, if desired. Display the pumpkins on a bulletin board titled "Welcome to Our Pretty Patterned Patch!"

VaReane Gray Heese
Springfield Elementary
Springfield, NE

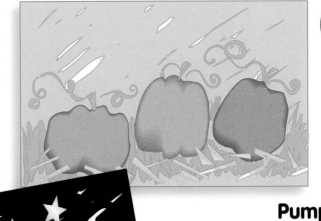

Pumpkin Paintings

Use these pumpkin patches to create a seasonal or holiday display! To begin, paint two or more pumpkins on a horizontally positioned 6" x 9" piece of white construction paper. After the paint dries, use crayons to illustrate a nighttime backdrop or a daytime setting. Use provided arts-and-crafts materials to complete the scene. For example, glue on construction paper cutouts to transform the pumpkins into jack-o'-lanterns, add adhesive foil stars to a nighttime sky, or glue on short lengths of raffia to resemble straw. It looks like fall!

adapted from an idea by Alyssa Weller
South School
Glencoe, IL

Pumpkins With Personality

Transforming paper lunch bags into pumpkin personalities is easy and fun! Using a ruler and alternating between two different colors of crayons, draw vertical and horizontal lines on the front and back of a white lunch bag. Cut out desired facial features from construction paper and glue them in place (be sure to allow room to fold down the top of the bag). Partially fill the bag with crumpled newspaper; then fold and staple the top closed. Near the fold tape a few lengths of curled ribbon for vines. Finally, add a green paper stem.

Fall Suncatchers

Make your school windows the talk of the town! In October, adorn school windows with a glowing display of pumpkin personalities. When November arrives, replace the pumpkins with colorful cornucopias.

Materials for one suncatcher:
8" square white paper
8" square clear Con-Tact covering
masking tape
small tissue paper squares in desired colors

Steps:
1. On the white paper, arrange tissue paper squares to create a desired design.
2. Remove the backing from the Con-Tact covering. Keeping the sticky side up, lay the covering on your work surface and secure the corners with tape.
3. Transfer the tissue paper design to the clear covering. Then replace the backing and remove the tape.
4. To display the resulting suncatcher, remove the backing and adhere the project to the inside of a window.
5. To remove the project, simply peel it from the window. For transport home, either adhere the project to its original backing or mount it atop an eight-inch paper square.

Sarah Winther Shumaker
Dover South Elementary School
Dover, OH

Frankenstein Look-Alikes

Students are sure to have a monstrously good time making and using these seasonal storage containers! *(Before you introduce the project, use a pointed instrument, such as the pointed end of a pair of scissors, to make two holes in each child's container for bolts.)*

Materials for one project:
18-oz. oatmeal container with lid
white tempera paint
green tempera paint
dishwashing liquid
paintbrush
2 hex head bolts with nuts
6" square of black felt
permanent black marker
construction paper scraps
scrap of silver gift wrap (or foil)
craft glue
scissors
rubber band

Steps:

1. **For the head,** mix white paint and green paint until a desired color is achieved. Add a squirt of dishwashing liquid (to keep dried paint from cracking). Then remove the container lid and paint the outside of the container. Set it aside to dry.

2. **To attach the bolts,** poke a bolt through each teacher-made hole. Then reach inside the container and thread a nut onto each bolt, securing it in place.

3. **For the hair,** use the marker to trace the outline of the lid in the center of the felt. Draw a wavy hairline about three-fourths of an inch outside the circle's perimeter. Cut the felt along the wavy outline. To attach the resulting hairpiece, snap the lid on the container. Spread craft glue on the felt inside the circle and run a trail of glue just outside the circle. Position the felt on the lid. Use the rubber band to hold the hair in place until the glue dries (see illustration).

4. **For the facial features,** cut two eyebrows from felt scraps, two eyes and a nose from construction paper, and a mouth from silver gift wrap. Use the marker to add details. Glue the cutouts in place.

Cindi Zsittnik, Denia Phillips, and Sherry Shank
Surrey School, Hagerstown, MD

Step 3

Bats in Flight

You'll generate plenty of enthusiasm right off the bat with these eerie nighttime scenes! Cut out a large construction paper moon and glue it on a 9" x 12" sheet of orange construction paper. To make the bat, cut two identical circles from black paper. Zigzag-cut one circle in half. Glue the two resulting wings to the remaining black circle. Next use construction paper scraps, glue, and a white crayon to add ears and facial features to the bat. Then glue the bat on the orange paper. Working atop a newspaper-covered surface, drip drops of thinned black tempera paint onto the project. Spread the paint drops by blowing briskly through a drinking straw. Oh, spooky!

Lisa Von Hatten
St. Paul Elementary
Highland, IL

Twinkle, Twinkle, Little Bat

Your youngsters will find these flashy fliers simply irresistible! To make a bat, use the pattern on page 85 to make a wing cutout from black construction paper. Trim a three-inch square of black felt into an oval and mount the resulting body in the center of the wings. From black construction paper, cut a 1½-inch circle (head), ears, and feet. Glue the paper ears and two wiggle eyes to the head; then add other desired facial features. Next glue the bat's head and feet to the project. Lastly use glitter glue to indicate an arm, a thumb, and four fingers on each bat wing. Mount the project on a 9" x 12" sheet of construction paper, add a bat fact, and display it on a bulletin board titled "Batty About Bats!"

Yolanda Matthews
Monrovia School
Huntsville, AL

A bat is a mammal.

Illuminating Cats

These wide-eyed kitties are "purrrrr-fect" for Halloween or anytime! Begin with two construction paper copies of the pattern on page 86. Cut out each shape; then cut along the dotted lines to make eyeholes. (Assist students with this step as needed.) On one cutout, use a crayon to draw the nose, whiskers, mouth, and legs of the cat. On the remaining cutout, lay a flat lollipop over each eyehole and secure the lollipop sticks with tape. Next, glue the two cutouts together, keeping the crayon features to the outside and the lollipops to the inside. Display the cute kitties in a window and watch their eyes glow!

Kristin Marple
St. Nicholas School
Egg Harbor, NJ

Indian Corn Napkin Rings

Add the perfect touch to any Thanksgiving table with colorful Indian corn napkin rings. Cut a supply of cardboard tubes into two-inch sections or rings. To make a napkin ring, tear individual two-inch squares of brown, yellow, red, black, orange, blue, and purple construction paper into small pieces. Then, in a mosaic pattern, glue the torn paper pieces on a two-inch ring. When the glue dries, tuck a napkin inside. Happy Thanksgiving!

Elizabeth Searls Almy
Greensboro, NC

Gobbler Greetings

These gorgeous gobblers are the perfect place for students to pen thankful thoughts for their loved ones.

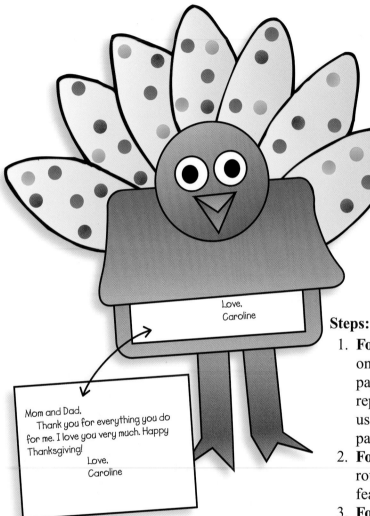

Mom and Dad,
   Thank you for everything you do for me. I love you very much. Happy Thanksgiving!
           Love,
           Caroline

Love,
Caroline

Materials for one card:
one 6" x 9" piece of yellow construction paper
one 6" x 9" piece of brown construction paper
one 3" brown construction paper circle
one 3" x 5" piece of white paper
two 1" x 5" orange construction paper strips
individual containers of red, green, and blue
   tempera paint
white, black, and orange paper scraps
3 cotton swabs
scissors
glue
pencil

Steps:

1. **For the tail feathers,** dip one end of a cotton swab in one paint color and repeatedly press it onto the yellow paper. Reload the swab as many times as desired. Then repeat the procedure for each remaining paint color, using a different cotton swab each time. When the painted paper is dry, cut several feather shapes from it.
2. **For the body,** fold the brown rectangle in half and round the corners. Keeping the fold at the top, glue the feathers to the back of the resulting body.
3. **For the head,** glue the brown circle to the body as shown. For facial features, cut two white eyes, two black pupils, and an orange diamond shape (for the beak) from paper scraps. Fold the diamond in half to create a beak. Glue the cutouts in place.
4. **For the legs and feet,** use a zigzag cut to trim one end of each orange paper strip. Then fold up the notched end of each paper strip to make a foot. Glue the legs to the body.
5. **To complete the card,** write a Thanksgiving message on the white paper. Unfold the body and glue the paper inside.

Elizabeth Searls Almy
Greensboro, NC

Turkey Windsock

The sight of these fine-feathered windsocks dancing in the breeze is sure to delight Thanksgiving enthusiasts of all ages!

Materials for one windsock:
one 4½" x 12" strip of brown construction paper
one 4" x 7" piece of orange construction paper
one 5" x 8" piece of red construction paper
one 6" x 9" piece of brown construction paper
one 2" x 6" piece of brown construction paper
black construction paper scrap (for eyes)
six 18" lengths of fall-colored crepe paper
one 20" length of yarn
scissors
glue
hole puncher

Step 2

Steps:
1. **To make the body,** roll the 4½" x 12" strip of brown paper into a large cylinder and glue the overlapping edges together. Set it aside to dry.
2. **To make the tail feathers,** trim the orange paper as shown. Glue the cutout atop the red paper. Trim the red paper to create an eye-catching border. Glue this cutout atop the brown paper and then trim the brown paper.
3. **For the head,** trim the 2" x 6" piece of brown paper into a desired shape. Cut two black eyes, a red wattle, and an orange diamond (for the beak) from the paper scraps. Fold the diamond in half and then glue the facial features in place.
4. **To assemble the turkey,** glue the tail feathers to the body (cylinder), covering the paper seam. Glue the head to the front of the body. Then glue the strips of crepe paper inside the lower rim of the project.
5. **To prepare the project for hanging,** punch two holes near the top of the tail feathers. Thread the yarn through the holes and securely tie the yarn ends.

Rita Arnold
Alden Hebron Grade School
Hebron, IL

Fantastic Feathers

To make one of these gobblers, use red, yellow, brown, and orange fingerpaints to paint an eight-inch square of tagboard. To make the turkey's body and head, use brown paper to cover one and one-half cardboard tubes. When the painted tagboard is dry, trim it to create a set of tail feathers. Then glue the paper-covered tubes to the feathers. Cut out two eyes, a beak, and a wattle from construction paper scraps and glue the cutouts in place. Attach construction paper feet, and this gobbler is ready to strut its stuff!

Laura LaPerna
Tedder Elementary
Pompano Beach, FL

Tissue-Paper Turkeys

Check out the fancy feathers on this gorgeous gobbler! Cut a supply of one-inch squares from brown, yellow, orange, red, green, blue, and purple tissue paper. Make a turkey cutout using the pattern on page 87. Glue a different color of overlapping tissue-paper squares to cover each tail feather. Next, glue brown overlapping tissue-paper squares to cover the head and body areas. To make eyes, feet, a beak, and a wattle, ball up individual tissue-paper squares in desired colors and glue them to the project in the appropriate places. Now that's one fine fowl!

Jan Minter
St. Pius V School
Long Beach, CA

Festive Wreaths

Personalized wreaths make precious holiday gifts! To begin, glue a seven-inch circle of gold foil gift wrap in the center of a 14-inch cardboard circle. Punch two holes side by side near the outer edge of the cardboard. Keeping the holes at the top of the circle, sketch a desired holiday design on the cardboard and program it for color. Fill in the design with tissue paper squares. To apply the tissue, wrap each square around the eraser end of a pencil, dip it in glue, and press it onto the cardboard. (This process takes several days.) Next, hot-glue a photo in the center of the foil. To ready the wreath for hanging, thread a length of colorful ribbon through the holes and securely tie the ribbon ends.

Maureen Glennon
Faller School
Ridgecrest, CA

Star of David

Brighten your Hanukkah festivities with the glow of this colorful Star of David. Prepare a tagboard tracer of the triangle pattern on page 88. Position the top point of the tracer near the top of a ten-inch square of yellow construction paper. Trace inside and outside the shape, and then flip the tracer so the top point is near the bottom of the yellow paper. Adjust the tracer as needed to make a six-pointed star; then trace inside and outside the tracer. Color each section of the resulting star a shade of blue or green. Then cut out the star, leaving a narrow border of yellow around the outer edge. Glue the cutout to dark blue paper. Cut out the shape again, this time leaving a narrow border of blue. Happy Hanukkah!

Elizabeth Searls Almy
Greensboro, NC

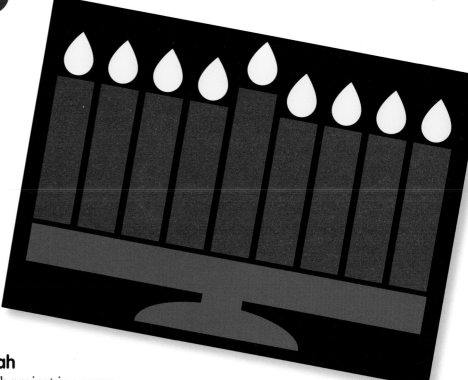

Glowing Menorah

The cheerful glow of this menorah project is a warm reminder of the great miracle it represents.

For each menorah you will need:

one 1" x 4" strip of red construction paper
eight 1" x 3" strips of red construction paper
nine 1" x 1½" pieces of yellow tissue paper
one 3" x 11" strip of blue construction paper
one 9" x 12" sheet of black construction paper

scissors
glue
pencil

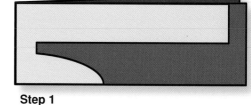

Step 1

Directions:

1. **For the menorah base,** fold the blue paper in half. Trace a template like the one shown on the folded paper; then cut along the outline. Glue the cutout near the bottom of the black paper.
2. **For the shammash,** glue the longest red strip slightly above the center of the base.
3. **For the eight candles,** glue four red strips on each side of the shammash, taking care to align the bottoms of the candles with the shammash.
4. **For the flames,** draw a flame atop the shammash and each candle. Carefully cut out each flame (provide assistance with this step as needed). Turn the project over. Drizzle glue around each flame cutout and press a piece of yellow tissue paper over the opening.
5. **Display** the completed project in a window for a glowing effect.

Rebecca Brudwick
Hoover Elementary School
North Mankato, MN

Old-Time Ornaments

These country-style ornaments are fun to make and oh, "sew" cute!

Materials for one ornament:
star or heart pattern (page 89)
brown paper lunch bag
2 cotton balls
1" square of cotton fabric
button
7" length of yarn or jute
scissors
tape
glue
fine-tip marker

Steps:

1. Trace the pattern on the unopened bag. Cut out the tracing, cutting through all layers, to make two cutouts. Discard the scraps.
2. On one side of each cutout, use a marker to draw stitches along the edge.
3. Turn one cutout with stitches face-down. To make a hanger, loop a length of yarn or jute and tape the ends to the cutout as shown. Stretch the two cotton balls and set the cotton in the center of the cutout.
4. Squeeze a line of glue along the edge of the cutout. Place the second cutout on top with stitches faceup. Gently press the edges to seal them.
5. Glue on a fabric square and button for decoration.

Rosana Sanchez
Arrey, NM

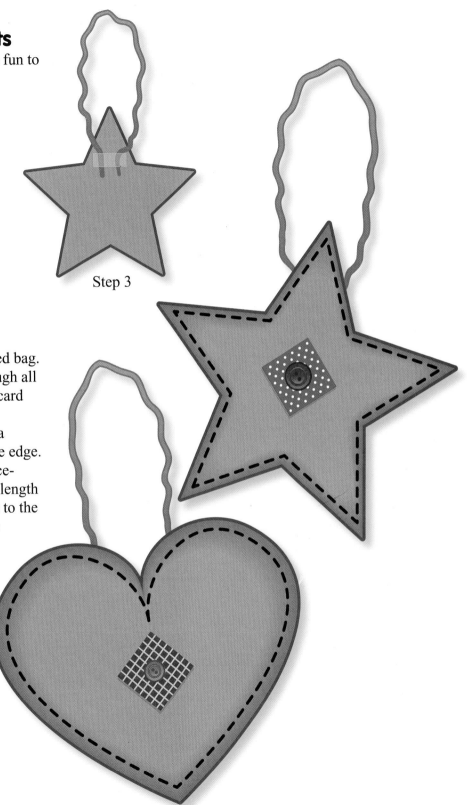

Step 3

25

Nifty Nutcrackers

A lineup of these stately soldiers is a sight to see! Plan to drop a few wrapped candies inside each nutcracker before it's carried home for the holidays!

Materials for one project:

empty Pringles potato crisps can with lid
3" x 10" strip of blue construction paper
2" x 10" strip of black construction paper
1" x 10" strip of black construction paper
2" x 10" strip of skin-toned construction paper
2" x 10" strip of red construction paper
two 1" squares of skin-toned construction paper
two 1" x 2" pieces of red construction paper

2 wiggle eyes
1 pom-pom (for nose)
4 small buttons
construction paper scraps
sequins
black marker
scissors
craft glue

Steps:

1. Remove the lid from the can. Gather the ten-inch paper strips. Set the narrower black strip aside. Starting at the lower edge of the can, glue the remaining strips to the can in the following order: blue, red, skin-toned, black. Keep the seams aligned at what will become the back of the project.
2. Glue the narrow black strip around the lower edge of the can, atop the blue strip. Align the seam.
3. Cut a hand shape from each skin-toned paper square. Glue one hand to one end of each 1" x 2" piece of red construction paper. Glue the resulting arms to opposite sides of the container.
4. Add facial features, buttons, and other desired details. Snap on the lid and the nutcracker is ready to strut his stuff!

Denia Phillips, Sherry Shank,
    and Cindi Zsittnik
Surrey School
Hagerstown, MD

Gingerbread Homes

These cozy cottages are deliciously fun to make! Partially fill a brown paper lunch bag with crumpled newspaper. Fold back the top of the bag and staple it. Use construction paper scraps, crayons, glue, and a hole puncher (optional) to add a roof, windows, a front door, and an abundance of scrumptious-looking decorations. Now that's home, sweet home!

Mara Bartusek
Fairview Elementary
Mora, MN

A Gingerbread Glyph

Try as you might, you won't find a more unique gingerbread project than this one! Make available the following colors of construction paper scraps: pink, blue, white, orange, red, green, yellow, purple, and black. Each student also needs a large paper cutout of a gingerbread pal, glue, scissors, crayons or markers, a pencil, and a copy of "Gingerbread Decorations" on page 90. A student completes page 90 by following the provided instructions; then she uses the resulting code to make hair, buttons, stripes, and facial features to glue on her gingerbread cutout. Display the completed projects and an enlarged version of page 90 on a bulletin board titled "A Gingerbread Who's Who."

Bonnie Hansen
Ashton Elementary
Sarasota, FL

Peppermint Paintings

Pour red tempera paint into a small container and then mix in a few drops of peppermint extract. Cut a piece of white paper to fit in an empty box or a box lid. Set the paper inside, dribble a small amount of paint on top, and then drop in a marble. Tilt the container to roll the marble through the paint until a desired effect is achieved. Then remove the marble and allow the paint to dry.

Next, remove the painting. Trace a candy cane pattern (page 91) on the back of it a desired number of times. Cut out each tracing. Then use each unique candy cane as desired. For example, hole-punch the top of it and secure a length of string to it as shown to make a gift tag; then address and sign the back of it. Or to create an ornament, mount the cutout on construction paper and add a hanger.

Sara Humiston
Lawrence, KS

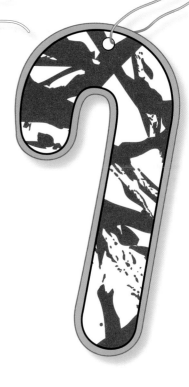

Irresistible Reindeer

Using templates of the reindeer face and heart-shaped antler patterns on pages 92 and 93, trace one face and two antlers onto one-inch graph paper. Alternating between two shades of brown, color the squares on each shape. Cut out the shapes and glue them onto brown construction paper. Then trim the brown paper to create a narrow border around each shape. Next, glue the antlers to the face and attach construction paper facial features and cutouts to resemble a sprig of holly. Put these reindeer on display, and you'll have plenty of passersby stopping to check out the handsome team!

Doris Hautala
Washington Elementary School
Ely, MN

Simply Santa

These Santa mobiles are sure to spread holiday cheer!

Materials for one mobile:

two 12" construction paper triangles
3" x 7" piece of skin-toned construction paper
6" x 9" piece of red construction paper
1½" x 12" piece of white construction paper
white, pink, and black construction paper scraps
several white cotton balls
four 16" lengths of red or green streamers
glue
scissors
black marker
hole puncher
string

Steps:

1. Glue the skin-toned construction paper approximately three inches from the top of a red triangle, as shown, to make a face. Trim the excess skin-toned paper.
2. Cut hat trim and a pom-pom from the white paper. Glue them in place. Cut away any excess hat trim.
3. Glue the white construction paper strip along the bottom edge of the project. Trim the ends.
4. Cut two triangles from the 6" x 9" piece of red paper to make arms. Glue them onto the back of the project. Cut mittens from the black construction paper. Glue them on.
5. Use a marker and pink construction paper to make eyes and a nose as shown.
6. Stretch the cotton balls. Glue them onto the project to make a beard.
7. Glue one end of each streamer onto the back of the project near the bottom edge. Glue the remaining triangle onto the back of the project, aligning the edges.
8. Use a hole puncher and string to make a hanger.

Doris Hautala
Washington Elementary
Ely, MN

Step 1

29

Torn-Paper Santa

To make a Santa, tear a beard shape from a 7" x 9" rectangle of white construction paper. Next, tear the edges from a 3" x 6" rectangle of skin-toned construction paper and glue the resulting face near the top of the beard as shown. Tear a hat shape from an eight-inch square of red construction paper and glue it above the face. Tear the edges from a 3" x 9" strip of white construction paper and glue the resulting hat band over the lower edge of the hat. Next fold the top of the hat to one side and glue a cotton ball to the tip. Then cut eyes and a nose from construction paper scraps and glue them on the face.

Lisa Strieker
St. Paul Elementary
Highland, IL

Jolly Santa

Nestled among this Santa's whiskers is a hearty "ho ho ho!"

Materials for one project:

12" square of skin-toned paper	scissors
4" x 12" strip of red construction paper	glue
1" x 12" strip of white construction paper	pencil

2½" x 8" strip of white construction paper
2" square of white paper
½" x 3" white construction paper strips for whiskers
construction paper scraps for eyes, nose, and mouth

Steps:

1. **For the face,** cut a large heart shape from the skin-toned paper.
2. **For the hat,** trace the pointed end of the heart onto the red paper. Cut out the hat and glue it atop the heart cutout. Glue the 1" x 12" strip of white paper to the bottom edge of the hat. Trim each end of the resulting hatband. Cut a hat ball from the two-inch white square. Glue it on the hat.
3. **For the facial features and mustache,** cut eyes, a nose, and a mouth from the construction paper scraps. Fold the eight-inch strip of white paper in half to four inches. Draw half of a mustache shape on the paper as shown. Cut on the outline and unfold the cutout. Glue the cutouts on the heart.
4. **For the whiskers,** roll each of several ½" x 3" white paper strips around a pencil. Slide the rolled paper off the pencil and glue one end to Santa's face. Continue until a desired number of whiskers are in place.

Step 2

Step 3

Doris Hautala
Washington Elementary
Ely, MN

Creative Christmas Tree

The sky is the limit when students take a multimedia approach to decorating poster-board Christmas trees! Give each child a simple tree shape cut from a 9" x 12" rectangle of poster board (or cardboard). Provide a wide assortment of craft supplies that includes construction paper, scissors, glue, tempera paints, paintbrushes, yarn, fabric scraps, foil stars, gift wrap, crayons, and markers. Each student shapes his tree (if desired), then picks and chooses from the provided supplies to decorate a tree that's fit for the season.

Joan Mary Macey
Binghamton City School District
Binghamton, NY

Perfectly Shaped Evergreen

Here's a "tree-mendous" project that pairs geometry and art! To prepare, cut two 1½" x 12" green construction paper strips. Cut each strip into 1½-inch squares. Then cut five squares in half diagonally to make ten triangles.

Next, position a 9" x 12" sheet of construction paper horizontally. Use a ruler to draw a line across the paper near the bottom edge. Then glue four squares side by side on the line, leaving space at either end of the row. Glue three squares in a row centered directly above the first row. Use two squares to make the next row and one square to make a fourth row. Glue one triangle at the top and four triangles on each side to form a tree as shown. If desired, use a hole puncher and construction paper scraps to make a number of small decorations; then glue them onto the tree.

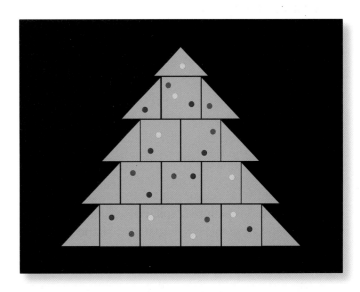

Rita Arnold
Alden Hebron Elementary School
Hebron, IL

Beautiful Bell

Ring in the holidays with a stained-glass look-alike! In advance, cut a supply of colorful tissue paper into approximately one-inch squares. To begin, cut along the outer lines of a white construction paper copy of the bell pattern on page 94. Place the bell on a piece of waxed paper or another nonstick surface. Using a paintbrush and liquid starch, adhere overlapping tissue-paper squares to the bell. Decorate the entire bell in this manner; then allow it to dry overnight.

After the bell is dry, trim any excess tissue paper. Cut out a second copy of the bell pattern, including the three inner sections. Trace the resulting bell frame on a 9" x 12" sheet of black construction paper. Carefully cut out the tracing. Glue the tracing atop the decorated bell, taking care to align the edges.

Maureen Glennon
Faller Elementary
St. Ridgecrest, CA

Kwanzaa Windsock

Herald the arrival of Kwanzaa with a striking windsock fashioned from traditional holiday colors.

Materials:
one 6" x 18" strip of black construction paper
one 2" x 18" strip of red construction paper
one 2" x 18" strip of green construction paper
six 16" strips of black crepe paper
one 36" length of black yarn
glue
hole puncher

Steps:
1. Glue the red and green strips to the black paper as shown.
2. When the glue has dried, roll the project into a cylinder and glue the overlapping edges together.
3. Glue one end of each crepe paper strip underneath the green rim.
4. Punch two holes opposite each other near the top of the black rim.
5. Thread each end of the yarn length through a different hole and securely tie it.

Kwanzaa Greeting

Foster an important Kwanzaa concept—that holiday gifts and decorations be created rather than purchased—by inviting students to make handcrafted cards for the holiday. To make a card like the one shown, glue an 8" x 11" sheet of black construction paper in the center of a 9" x 12" sheet of red construction paper. When the glue is dry, fold the paper in half, keeping the black paper to the outside. Next, fashion a Kwanzaa symbol from construction paper scraps. (See "Seven Symbols of Kwanzaa" on this page.) Glue the symbol, a greeting, and any additional decorations desired on the front of the resulting card. On a 2" x 8" strip of white paper, name and briefly describe the featured symbol. Then, on a 4½" x 6" rectangle of white paper, write, sign, and decorate a holiday message. Glue the programming inside the card as shown, and the greeting is ready to deliver!

Seven Symbols of Kwanzaa

Mkeka *(m-KAY-kah)* A woven mat that represents tradition and on which all other symbols are placed.

Mazao *(mah-ZAH-oh)* A basket or bowl of fruits and vegetables that represents the harvest and the rewards of working together.

Muhindi *(moo-HEEN-dee)* Ears of corn that represent children and the future.

Zawadi *(zah-WAH-dee)* Gifts that are given as acts of sharing and labors of love.

Kinara *(kee-NAH-rah)* A candleholder (for seven candles) that represents African ancestors.

Mishumaa Saba *(mee-shoo-MAH SAH-ba)* Seven candles (three red, three green, and one black) that represent the seven principles of Kwanzaa.

Kikombe cha Umoja *(kee-KOHM-bay chah oo-MOH-jah)* A unity cup that represents the togetherness of family and community.

The First Snow

To begin, peel the sticker from one end of a plastic thread spool and pour a thin layer of white tempera paint into a shallow container. Then repeatedly dip the uncovered end of the thread spool into the white paint and press it onto a 9" x 12" sheet of dark blue construction paper. When a desired effect is achieved, sprinkle the flurry of snowflakes with clear or silver glitter. Shake off the excess glitter and allow drying time. To create window panes, glue three ½" x 9" paper strips and three ½" x 12" paper strips onto the project as pictured. Let it snow!

Rebecca Brudwick
North Mankato, MN

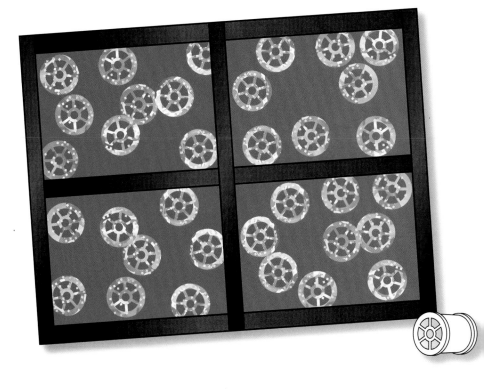

Sparkly Snowflakes

Create a flurry of wintry decorations! To make one snowflake ornament, stack and glue three craft sticks—one atop the other—to form a snowflake shape similar to the one shown. Glue puzzle pieces along the length of each stick. Allow the glue to dry. Use white acrylic paint to paint the front and back of the ornament. After the paint dries, squeeze lines of glue on the front. Sprinkle on glitter and then gently shake off any excess. To make a hanger, knot the ends of a length of metallic thread. Use a generous amount of glue to attach it to the back of the ornament.

Maureen Glennon
Faller Elementary
St. Ridgecrest, CA

Snowflake Mobile

Create a flurry of delicate snowflakes without waiting for the weather to cooperate! To make a three-dimensional snowflake, stack three 4" x 5½" pieces of blank white paper. Fold the stack in half and crease; then unfold the stack, staple twice along the fold line, and refold. Cutting through all thicknesses, sculpt the folded paper as desired, taking extra care to not cut away the staples. Finally, unfold the paper and separate the layers to reveal a 3-D flake. Suspend the project in the classroom from a length of monofilament line. Or create three snowflakes and use varying lengths of monofilament line to suspend them from a 3" x 6" strip of tagboard as shown. Let it snow, let it snow, let it snow!

Elizabeth Searls Almy
Greensboro, NC

Snowy Marshmallow Painting

Use marshmallows to create a blizzard of painting possibilities! First, use construction paper and crayons to create a desired outdoor scene on a sheet of blue construction paper. Then pour a small amount of white tempera paint into a shallow container. Carefully insert a Popsicle stick into one end of a large marshmallow. Dip the marshmallow into the paint and then make prints on the artwork to create a snowy effect. Repeat the dipping-and-painting process until a desired effect is achieved. If desired, mount the dried painting on a slightly larger piece of construction paper to frame it.

Robin Bearden
Hiram Elementary
Hiram, GA

Snowflake Snowpal

You can sum up these snowpals with one word: unique! To make the body, fold a nine-inch white circle in half three times and make a series of desired cuts. Then unfold the paper and glue a four-inch white circle (head) to the top of the body. Add desired facial features. Next cut out a paper scarf and hat for the snowpal. Use markers or crayons to brightly color the clothing cutouts, creating a striped or checkered pattern if desired. Glue the clothing to the project and the snowpal is ready to display.

Mary Napoli
Swiftwater, PA

Stand-Up Snowpals

Students will have loads of frosty fun building these stand-up snowpals, even in sunny weather! To make a snowpal, fold in half four 6" x 9" pieces of white construction paper (to 3" x 9"). Trace a tagboard template of the pattern from page 95 onto each piece of folded paper. Cut along the outlines and unfold each cutout. Use crayons or permanent markers to decorate each resulting snowpal. Then refold each snowpal, keeping the decorations to the inside. Also cut a branchlike arm from each of four 1" x 4" strips of brown construction paper.

To assemble the project, spread glue on the top surface of one folded snowpal. Align a second folded snowpal atop the glue, sandwiching the end of one arm between the surfaces. In the same manner, glue a third snowpal to the second snowpal, and the fourth snowpal to the third snowpal. Then pick up the project and glue the top and bottom surfaces together, sandwiching the last arm cutout between them. For a truly frosty snowpal, mix together equal amounts of Epsom salts and water, paint all four sides of the snowpal, and set it aside to dry.

Linda P. Lovelace
Halifax, VA

Cool Carriers

Store sight word cards, flash cards, or cards of any kind in these snazzy snowpal carriers!

Materials for one project:

9" white construction paper circle
9" white construction paper semicircle
2 colorful earmuff patterns (page 96)
orange nose pattern (page 96)
2 wiggle eyes
2" x 12" length of colorful fabric

two 12" pipe cleaners
hole puncher
stapler
crayons or markers
scissors
glue

Steps:

1. **For the pocket,** run a trail of glue around the curved edge of the semicircle and then align the semicircle atop the circle.

2. **For the handle,** punch two holes in the carrier as shown. Securely hook one end of one pipe cleaner through each hole. Twist together the two unattached ends.

3. **For the scarf,** flip the carrier over. Keeping the handle at the top, staple the middle of the fabric strip near the bottom of the circle. Knot the fabric and fringe-cut the ends.

4. **For the earmuffs,** cut out the patterns and add desired details. Glue them in place.

5. **For facial features,** cut out the nose pattern. Glue the nose cutout and wiggle eyes in place. Draw a big smile—the carrier is ready!

adapted from an idea by Linda Maitland
Libby Elementary
Carthage, TX

Step 2

Snowpal Snack Bag

What goes thumpity, thump, thump—poppity, pop, pop?
A snowpal snack bag that's filled to the brim with popcorn!

Materials:

one resealable sandwich bag
one 5" x 6" piece of white paper
one 5" x 8" piece of black construction paper
green, orange, and black construction paper scraps
two blue ¾" dot stickers
eight red ¾" dot stickers
scissors
crayons
glue
popcorn

Directions:

1. Slip the white paper inside the sandwich bag.
2. Cut a hat shape from the black paper.
3. Cut two holly leaves from green paper and add desired crayon details. Glue the leaves to the hat and add three red dot stickers (holly berries).
4. On the front of the bag, run a trail of craft glue approximately one-half inch below the seal. Firmly press the hat atop the glue.
5. Cut out an orange carrot-shaped nose and two black eyebrows.
6. Attach facial features to the bag as shown.
7. When the project is dry, open the bag and pour popcorn behind the white paper.

Melanie Miller
Nashport, OH

Snowpal Magnets

To make one snowpal magnet, use white acrylic paint to paint a wooden ice-cream spoon. After the paint is dry, cut a top hat from black paper. With the spoon positioned so that the narrow part is at the top, glue on the hat. Tie a length of ribbon around the stick to make a scarf. Then use fine-tip permanent markers to draw on two eyes, a nose, a mouth, and buttons. Next, cut two branchlike arms from construction paper. Turn the project over. Glue on the arms. Then adhere a strip of magnetic tape to the back of the project.

adapted from an idea by Kristy Peltier
Kingsley Elementary
Kingsport, TN

Paper Bag Snowpal

Your youngsters will have a flurry of frosty fun creating these three-dimensional snowpals!

Materials for one snowpal:

paper lunch bag

masking tape

newspaper cut into strips

wallpaper paste

rubber band

white tempera paint

buttons, construction paper scraps, pipe cleaner piece
   (facial features and accessories)

paintbrush

5" black construction paper circle (hat)

3" x 12" strip of black construction paper (hat)

glue

18" strip of fabric (scarf)

2 twigs (arms)

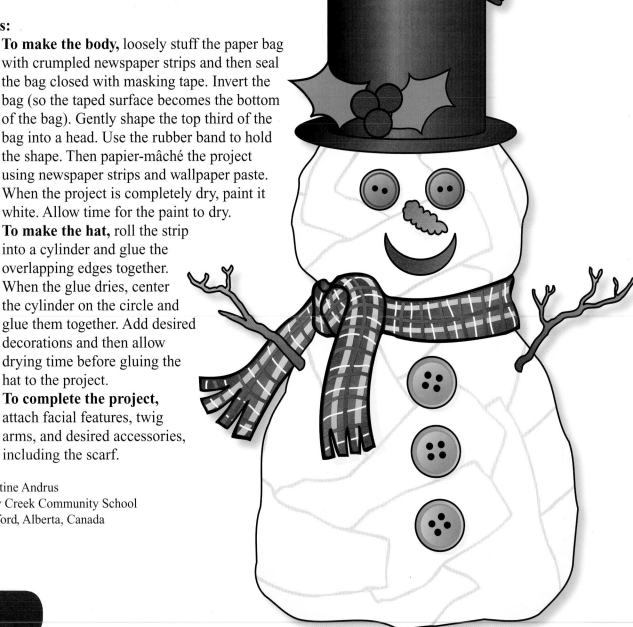

Steps:

1. **To make the body,** loosely stuff the paper bag with crumpled newspaper strips and then seal the bag closed with masking tape. Invert the bag (so the taped surface becomes the bottom of the bag). Gently shape the top third of the bag into a head. Use the rubber band to hold the shape. Then papier-mâché the project using newspaper strips and wallpaper paste. When the project is completely dry, paint it white. Allow time for the paint to dry.

2. **To make the hat,** roll the strip into a cylinder and glue the overlapping edges together. When the glue dries, center the cylinder on the circle and glue them together. Add desired decorations and then allow drying time before gluing the hat to the project.

3. **To complete the project,** attach facial features, twig arms, and desired accessories, including the scarf.

Christine Andrus
Berry Creek Community School
Cessford, Alberta, Canada

Snazzy Snow Globe

Create a flurry of excitement with these handcrafted snow globes. To make a snow globe, cut an eight-inch circle from light blue construction paper and an eight-inch half circle from white construction paper. Trim the straight edge of the half circle to resemble fallen snow; then glue this cutout atop the blue circle. Next use construction paper scraps, a hole puncher, glue, and crayons or markers to create a snowy scene. When the glue is dry, wrap the project with clear plastic wrap. Use clear tape to secure the plastic wrap to the back of the project. To make the snow globe's base, trace the outline of a protractor (or something similar) onto brown or black paper, and cut along the resulting outline. Glue the plastic-covered project to the base.

Festive Timelines

In celebration of Dr. Martin Luther King Jr.'s birthday (the third Monday in January), have each child make a festive four-event timeline of his life. To make a timeline, fold a 3" x 12" strip of drawing paper in half twice; then unfold the paper to reveal four equal sections. Leaving a half-inch margin at the top of the strip and working in chronological order from left to right, label each section with a different event.

Accordion-fold the strip and decorate the front of the folded project to resemble a birthday cake. Next, cut out four candle flames from scrap paper and glue them to the tops of four ½" x 2" construction paper strips to make lit candles. Unfold the timeline and glue one candle to the top of each section, positioning the candles so that when the project is refolded, each one is visible.

In 1929 Martin Luther King Jr. was born in Atlanta, Georgia.

In 1953 Martin got married to Coretta Scott.

In 1963 he gave a speech in Washington, DC, about his dream for the future.

In 1968 Martin Luther King Jr. was killed.

Happy Birthday, Dr. King!

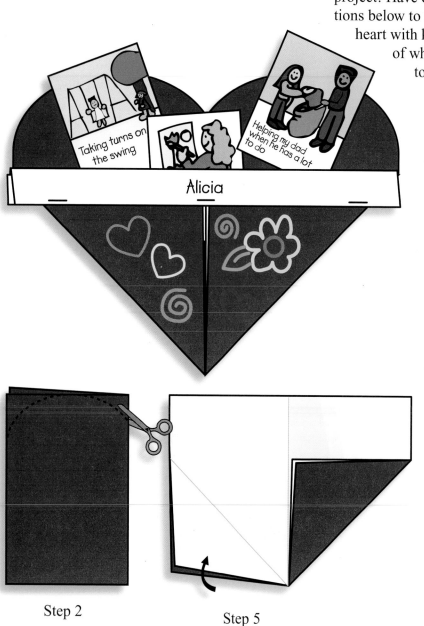

Alicia

Step 2

Step 5

Filled With Kindness

Promote thoughtful behavior with this Valentine's Day project! Have each student use the materials and directions below to make a heart-shaped pocket. To fill her heart with kindness, give the youngster a quarter sheet of white paper on each of several days. Ask her to illustrate and label a different example of kind behavior on each piece of paper. Then instruct her to store her work in her prepared pocket.

Materials for one project:
9" x 12" sheet of red construction paper
scissors
9" x 12" sheet of white construction paper
stapler
markers or crayons

Steps:
1. Fold the red paper in half to 6" x 9".
2. Cut the top to round it as shown. Unfold the paper.
3. Fold the white paper in half to 6" x 9". Unfold it.
4. Place the white paper atop the red paper, aligning the fold lines.
5. Fold up the bottom corners to the center.
6. Fold down the white paper to meet the red paper. Then carefully fold it over to make the top of the pocket.
7. Staple the pocket at both ends and in the middle.
8. Personalize the pocket as desired.

Judith Panzella
Public School #3
Cliffside Park, NJ

Sweet Cardholders

Candy look-alikes make these valentine holders irresistible! To make one, fold a 12" x 18" sheet of paper in half to 9" x 12". Fold down two inches of the top layer. Turn the project over and then fold down two inches of what is now the top layer. Staple the sides of the project together.

Next, use the pattern on page 97 to make a construction paper kiss cutout. Glue the kiss onto the dull side of a piece of aluminum foil. Then trim the excess foil. Snip a triangle from one end of a 1" x 5" white paper strip, as shown, and illustrate the strip with hearts. Glue the other end of the strip to the paper side of the chocolate kiss. Glue the kiss onto the left-hand side of the cardholder and sign your name.

adapted from an idea by Deborah Lockhart
William B. Tecler School
Amsterdam, NY

The Valentine Express

For speedy delivery of valentine wishes, "choo-choo-choose" the Valentine Express! Collect a class supply of clean and empty half-gallon juice cartons and then cut away the top and one side panel of each container. If desired, prewrap each child's container in red, pink, or white paper and brad four tagboard wheels in place. (Or assist students as they complete these steps.) Then set aside time for each child to personalize his boxcar. Display the completed projects in alphabetical order.

Karen Nelson
Smith School, Helena, MT

Bumblebee Valentines

These darling valentines are perfect for declaring, " 'Bee' Mine!"

Materials for one valentine:
small cardboard tube
4½" x 6" yellow construction paper rectangle
three 4" yellow construction paper squares
three 5" black construction paper squares
3" x 6" black construction paper rectangle
black construction paper scraps
fine-tip marker
clear tape
scissors
glue

Steps:

1. Squeeze a line of glue along the edges of the yellow rectangle. Wrap the paper around the cardboard tube.
2. Cut the black rectangle into three strips approximately 1" x 6" each. Glue them onto the tube to make stripes.
3. To make three hearts, fold each yellow square in half. Draw half of a heart along each fold as shown; cut it out.
4. Unfold each heart. Draw a face on one.
5. Glue each heart onto a black square. Trim the paper, leaving a narrow border.
6. To make wings, glue together the blank hearts as shown. Tape the wings to the tube.
7. To make a head, cut two antennae from the black paper scraps and glue them onto the back of the illustrated heart. Glue the head to the tube.

Pam Sartory
Palm Beach Gardens, FL

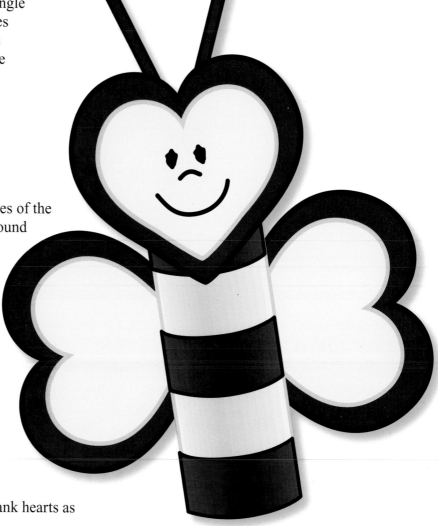

Step 1

Step 2

Step 3

Step 6

Heartfelt Messages

There's a "tree-mendous" amount of love in this valentine greeting! Fold a 12" x 18" sheet of white construction paper in half. Next, cut small heart shapes from red, pink, or purple construction paper. Arrange the hearts on the front of the card in the shape of a tree and glue them in place. Below the tree shape, glue a brown trunk and a planter shape cut from paper. When the glue is dry, use crayons or markers to add foliage and a Valentine's Day greeting. Inside the card, write a heartfelt message, add artwork, and sign your name. This handcrafted valentine greeting is sure to warm the heart of a loved one!

adapted from an idea by Mary Ann S. Jones
Clark Springs Elementary School
Richmond, VA

Patriotic Profiles

Showcase your youngsters' presidential dreams on these one-of-a-kind posters. In advance, have a parent volunteer (with the aid of an overhead projector) outline the shadow of each child's profile on a 12" x 18" sheet of white construction paper. To add color to her profile, a student uses a paint-brush and a minimal amount of water to "paint" yellow and blue tissue paper squares onto the shape. While her project is drying, she traces a heart-shaped template onto writing paper and writes her presidential dreams inside the resulting shape. Then she cuts out the shape, mounts it on red paper, and trims the red paper to form a narrow border.

When the student's profile is dry, she removes the tissue paper squares, cuts out the profile, and mounts it as she did the heart cutout. Then she glues both cutouts onto a 12" x 18" sheet of dark blue construction paper as shown and adds desired star cutouts.

adapted from an idea by Monica Millspaugh
Davis Elementary
Portland, OR

If I become president, I will live in the White House. I will travel to other countries to talk to their leaders. I will make the world peaceful.

A Lovable Lion

Whether March comes in like a lion or not, you're sure to get a roaring response to this project! To make a lion, color or paint a thin, nine-inch white paper plate yellow or light brown; then add facial features. To make the lion's mane, glue three-inch lengths of brown and yellow yarn (in an alternating fashion) around the entire plate rim. Finally, cut a pair of lion ears from brown paper and glue them in place.

Catherine Strickland
Myers Elementary School
Gainesville, GA

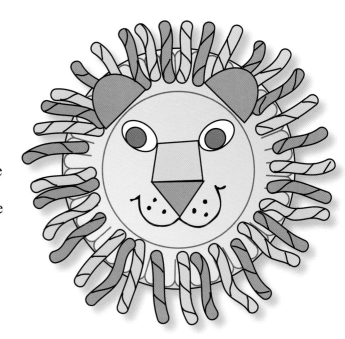

Woolly Lambs

With fleece as white as snow, these adorable lambs are perfect for the month of March!

Materials for one lamb:
6" white paper doily
8½" white paper circle
1 gray construction paper copy of the face and ear patterns on page 98
4" square of black construction paper
construction paper scrap for nose
cotton balls
black crayon
glue
scissors

Steps:
1. **To make the body,** gently pull apart cotton balls and glue them on the paper circle until it is completely covered.
2. **To make the head,** cut out the face and ear patterns. Cut a nose from scrap paper. Draw two eyes and a mouth on the face, and glue the nose in place. Then glue the face and ears on the doily.
3. **To make the legs,** fold the black paper square in half and cut out a leg shape.
4. **To assemble the project,** glue the head and legs to the body as shown.

adapted from an idea by Marsha Kathmann
South Kortright Central School
South Kortright, NY

High-Flying Mosaics

Batten down the hatches! A gust of kite-making creativity is in the forecast! Trace a kite-shaped template on a 12" x 18" sheet of construction paper, and cut along the resulting outline. Draw lines on the cutout as shown. Next, glue one-inch construction paper squares atop the cutout to create a desired design. For best results, work outward from where the lines cross and carefully align the construction paper squares. When the glue dries, trim around the original kite shape. Next, hole-punch the bottom corner of the kite. Thread one end of a length of twine through the hole and securely fasten it. Tie strips of colorful fabric or tissue paper to the kite string and the project is ready for display.

Jennifer Brahos
Mandan, ND

Colorful Kite

Brighten the classroom with these symmetrical fliers! To begin, fold a nine-inch construction paper square in half diagonally and then fold the resulting triangle in half. Unfold the paper and then position it so that one corner is at the top. In the top two sections, place dabs of tempera paint. Lift up the bottom corner to fold the paper in half diagonally again. Gently rub the top of the folded paper and then unfold it.

After the paint dries, use a permanent marker to trace the fold lines. Position another nine-inch construction paper square so that one corner is at the top. At the bottom, tape on two 18-inch lengths of crepe paper streamers. Glue the painted square on top, aligning the edges.

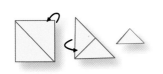

Green Pepper Prints

Your lads and lassies will smile upon this green pepper painting project! Plan to complete the project in two days.

On day one, cover a work surface with newspaper and pour a thin layer of green tempera paint into a shallow container. Cut away the top of a green pepper and then remove the insides from the pepper. Dip the cut end of the pepper into the paint and repeatedly press it onto white construction paper. Reload the pepper with paint as needed. Overlap the painted shapes as you cover the paper.

On day two, use green crayons in a variety of hues to color the unpainted areas of the paper. Then trace the shamrock pattern on page 99 on the back of the paper, cut along the resulting outline, and mount the cutout on a larger piece of colorful construction paper. Trim the colorful paper if desired.

adapted from an idea by Linda Masternak Justice
Kansas City, MO

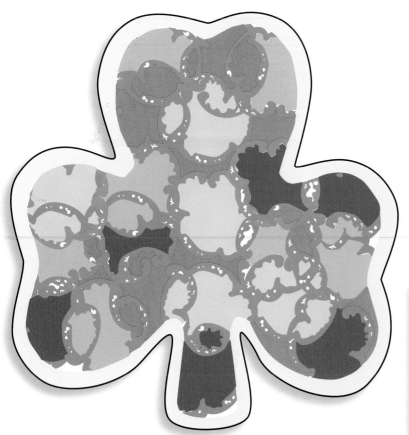

stamping technique

St. Patrick's Day Mobile

Dangle these spiraling mobiles around the classroom, and the luck of the Irish is sure to be nearby.

Materials for one mobile:
9" white paper plate
wide paintbrush
green watercolor paint
2 white construction paper copies of the
    St. Patrick's Day patterns on page 100
3' length of nylon monofilament line
hole puncher
crayons
scissors
glue

Steps:
1. Paint the top of the paper plate and then invert the plate and paint the bottom.
2. Color the patterns and cut them out.
3. Spread glue on the blank side of each pot-of-gold pattern; then press the glued surfaces together, sandwiching one end of the monofilament line between the shapes as shown.
4. Using the method described in Step 3, glue each remaining pair of cutouts to the line. Leave about two inches of empty line between pairs.
5. When the plate is dry, start at one edge and cut in a circular fashion to the center of the plate. Pull the resulting spiral upward and hole-punch the center.
6. Thread the monofilament line up through the center of the spiral and through the hole.
7. Pull the line through the hole until the cutouts are in a desired position and then securely tie the line to the top of the spiral.
8. Tie a loop at the top of the remaining line.
9. Suspend the mobile where it's sure to spin in the breeze!

Linda P. Lovelace
Halifax, VA

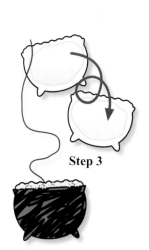

Step 3

Eggs Extraordinaire

Prepare pretty printed Easter eggs using pipe cleaners and paint! To begin, make a construction paper egg cutout (pattern on page 101). Bend pipe cleaner lengths into different shapes, fashioning a handle on each one. Dip one shape into a shallow container of paint and then repeatedly press it onto the egg. Reload as needed. Repeat the procedure with additional shapes and paint colors. (To use a pipe cleaner shape with more than one color of paint, rinse it clean and pat it dry with a paper towel.) When the prints are dry, display the egg shapes as desired.

Pretty Pasta Eggs

Textured and colorful, this appealing egg-decorating project is filled with "pasta-bilities"! Begin the project with a poster board egg cutout (pattern on page 101) and a supply of three different pasta shapes. Paint a layer of glue on one-third of the egg and then cover the area with one shape of pasta pieces. Repeat this step two times, using a different pasta shape each time. When the glue is dry, paint each third of the egg a different pastel color. Now that's an "eggs-tra" special egg!

Bunny Bags

Tuck a few treats into these student-made bags to top off your Easter festivities. "Every-bunny" is sure to love them!

Materials for one bunny bag:

white paper lunch bag
2 spring-type wooden clothespins
3" x 5" piece of white construction paper (outer ears)
2" x 4" piece of white construction paper (arms)
3" x 5" piece of white construction paper (feet)
2" x 4" piece of pink construction paper (inner ears)

construction paper scraps
black marker
cotton ball
glue
scissors
wrapped candies (optional)

Steps:

1. **For the bunny's body,** open the paper lunch bag and then fold down the top 2½ inches of the bag. Clip the clothespins to the fold.

2. **For the bunny's ears,** fold in half lengthwise one 3" x 5" piece of white paper and cut out two matching ear shapes. Fold in half lengthwise the 2" x 4" piece of pink paper and cut out two matching inner-ear shapes. Glue one pink cutout inside each white cutout. Glue each resulting ear to a clothespin.

3. **For the bunny's arms,** fold in half lengthwise the 2" x 4" piece of white paper and cut out two matching arm shapes. Fold one end of each arm cutout to create a tab. Glue each tab to the front of the bag as shown.

4. **For the bunny's feet,** fold in half the other 3" x 5" piece of white paper and cut out two matching foot shapes. Glue the feet to the bottom of the bag.

5. **For the bunny's face,** cut out eyes, a nose, and teeth from construction paper scraps. Glue the cutouts to the folded flap of the bag.

6. **To complete the bag,** use a marker to add desired details to the bunny's face, arms, and feet. Glue a cotton-ball tail to the back of the bag. Then, if desired, remove the bunny ears, carefully open the bag, and tuck a few Easter treats inside!

Mariko Layton
Johnstown, PA

Home, Tweet Home!

Even though these birdhouse windsocks are not ready for residents, they evoke plenty of fine-feathered thoughts!

Materials for one project:
6" x 18" strip of construction paper (for cylinder)
two 6" x 9" pieces of construction paper (for house)
four 1½" x 6" strips of construction paper (for house trim)
construction paper scraps
eight 16" strips of crepe paper
36" length of yarn
crayons or markers
hole puncher
scissors
glue

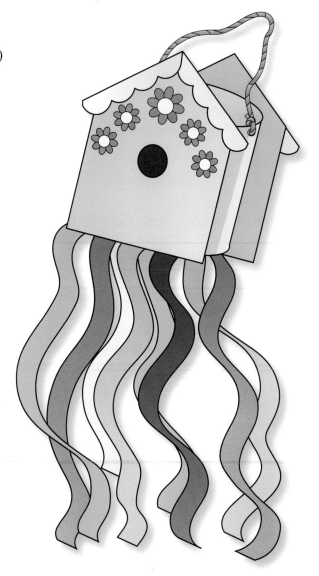

Steps:
1. Roll the 6" x 18" strip of paper into a cylinder and glue the overlapping edges together. Set it aside to dry.
2. To make the house shapes, trim away the top two corners of each 6" x 9" piece of paper. Cut a scalloped border along one six-inch edge of each 1½" x 6" paper strip. Glue the resulting trim to the house cutouts as shown. Embellish the house shapes with desired decorations.
3. Glue one house shape atop the cylinder's seam and the other house shape directly opposite it, keeping the decorations to the outside.
4. Glue the crepe paper strips inside the lower rim of the project.
5. At the top of the cylinder, punch two holes directly opposite each other.
6. Thread each end of the yarn length through a different hole and securely tie it.

Jill Putnam
Wheelock Primary School
Fredonia, NY

Country Duck

Check out this dapper duck! For a dandy spring-time display, suspend the little darlings from the classroom ceiling.

Materials for one duck:
tagboard templates of the patterns on
　　pages 102 and 103
9" x 12" sheet of white construction paper
three 4" squares of white construction paper
4" x 8" rectangle of yellow construction paper
4" x 6" rectangle of another color of
　　construction paper
assorted construction paper scraps
scissors
glue
2 large plastic buttons
hole puncher
24" length of yarn

Steps:

1. To make the body, trace the pattern on page 102 on the 9" x 12" white paper. Carefully tear around the outline.
2. Use the patterns on page 103 to trace two wings and one tail on the four-inch squares of white paper—one shape per square. Carefully tear around the outlines.
3. Use the patterns on page 103 to trace two feet and one bill on the yellow paper. Cut out the shapes. Overlap the outer corners of the bill and glue them together.
4. Trace the hat (pattern on page 103) on the 4" x 6" paper rectangle. Cut out the shape.
5. Assemble the pieces from Steps 1–4 as shown.
6. Glue two construction paper eyes in place and then use construction paper scraps and the buttons to finish decorating the duck.
7. Hole-punch the top of the hat. Thread one end of the yarn through the hole and tie it.

Linda Oesterle
Eggert Elementary School
Orchard Park, NY

Earth-Friendly Mobile

Just in time for Earth Day—a mobile with important messages about recycling!

Materials for one mobile:

metal hanger
2-page spread of newspaper,
  folded twice
copy of two of the mobile
  patterns on page 104
four 4" white construction paper circles
four 1' lengths of string or twine

crayons or markers
scissors
glue
hole puncher
small recyclable items

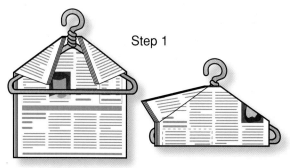

Steps:

1. Lay the hanger on the folded newspaper with the neck extending off the paper. Fold down the top corners of the paper and bring the lower edge upward, folding the lower corners over the top of the hanger (see below). Flip the hanger and glue the paper.

2. Color two of the patterns on page 104 and cut them out. Glue one pattern on each side of the wrapped hanger.

3. Illustrate a different recyclable item on each circle. Hole-punch the top of the circle; then flip it over and describe the item on the back.

4. Punch four holes along the bottom of the wrapped hanger. Use the string lengths to attach the illustrated circles to the hanger.

5. Glue small recyclables to the newspaper-covered hanger as desired.

Jeri Daugherity
Mother Seton School
Emmitsburg, MD

Step 1

Pretty Posies

With these flowers blooming in your classroom, there's no doubt that spring has sprung! Prepare containers of washable tempera paint in pastel colors. To make one blossom, use a paintbrush to paint the palm side of one hand. With fingers slightly outstretched, make a handprint on a piece of heavy white construction paper. Repeat or change colors to make one or two additional blossoms. Allow the prints to dry. Then trim the paper, leaving a white border around each print. Glue the prints onto a 12" x 18" sheet of construction paper. Add construction paper stems, folded leaf cutouts, and fringed construction paper grass.

Elise Miller
Montebello School
Phoenix, AZ

Touchable Tulips

Students will want to reach out and touch these terrific springtime tulips! To make the three-dimensional vase, roll a 4½" x 6" piece of construction paper into a cylinder and glue the overlapping edges together. When the glue dries, secure the seam of the vase near the bottom of an 8" x 11" sheet of colorful construction paper. Next trace a tulip-shaped template (patterns on page 105) onto a colorful party napkin three times. Cut out the shapes. With the napkin design facedown, use a small drop of glue to attach a cotton ball to the center of each tulip cutout. Next squeeze a thin trail of glue around the perimeter of each cutout. Turn over each tulip and secure it above the vase as shown. Cut out green paper stems and leaves and glue them in place. Mount the completed project atop a 9" x 12" sheet of contrasting construction paper.

Elizabeth Searls Almy
Greensboro, NC

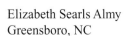

Soda-Bottle Blossoms

Paint a beautiful bouquet of springtime blossoms using the bottom of an individual-sized plastic soda bottle! To make a vase, fold a six-inch square of construction paper in half and trim it as shown. Unfold the cutout and glue it near the lower edge of a vertically positioned 12" x 18" sheet of construction paper. Pour a thin layer of tempera paint into a shallow container. Dip the bottom of a plastic soda bottle into the paint and repeatedly press it onto the construction paper to make a desired number of blossoms. Reapply the paint on the bottle as needed. When the paint dries, use a circular sponge to paint the center of each blossom, or glue construction paper or pom-pom centers in place. Then use a green marker to draw stems.

Sonja Stoll
Summerfield Elementary School
Summerfield, KS

Fluffy Dandelions

These dandelion look-alikes confirm that spring has sprung! To begin, cut three stems and several leaves from green paper. Glue the cutouts to a 9" x 12" sheet of dark blue construction paper. Next, glue a narrow strip of fringed green paper to the lower edge of the project to resemble grass. To make the fluffy dandelion heads, dot a circle of glue at the top of each stem; then pull tiny tufts from a cotton ball and press them into the glue. If desired, glue a few tufts blowing in the breeze.

Elizabeth Searls Almy
Greensboro, NC

Flowers for Mother's Day

Loved ones will bloom with pride when they receive these colorful Mother's Day mementos.

Materials for one:
green construction paper:
  9" x 12" sheet
  eight ½" x 2½" strips
colorful construction paper
  scraps
scissors
crayons
glue

Steps:

1. Fold the large green paper into thirds lengthwise (prefold if desired). Unfold it.
2. Fold the top edge of the paper to the top fold line and then unfold the paper and reverse-fold it.
3. Fold the bottom edge of the paper to the bottom fold line and then unfold the paper and reverse-fold it.
4. Fringe-cut the bottom edge of the paper, being careful to not cut through the closest fold line.
5. Spread glue over the midsection of the paper. Bring the top fold and the bottom fold together in the center of the glued surface as shown. Set the paper aside to dry.
6. Cut out eight flower shapes from colorful construction paper scraps. Use a crayon to write one letter from the phrase "I love you" on each flower. Glue each flower cutout to a green construction paper strip.
7. Glue the back of each flower stem to the uncut lip of the green paper. Carefully bend the fringed edges forward for added effect.

Elizabeth Searls Almy
Greensboro, NC

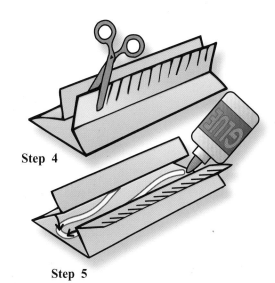

Step 4

Step 5

Handmade Butterflies

Delight moms and other significant women in your students' lives with handcrafted tokens of love! Paint the palm side of a child's hands a desired color. Keeping his thumbs aligned and his fingers spread, he presses his painted hands onto a 9" x 12" sheet of white construction paper. When the paint dries, he uses markers or crayons to draw and color the body and antennae of the resulting butterfly, and to write a desired greeting. Next he colors a copy of the poem on page 106, cuts it out, and glues it on the back of his project. He adds desired decorations with markers or crayons; then he signs his name.

Paula Stewart
Nathanael Greene Academy
Siloam, GA

Beautiful Butterflies

Students jump into this butterfly project with both feet! To make the butterfly's wings, a youngster stands on a sheet of white construction paper so that his shoe-clad feet are side by side and touching. He asks a classmate to trace around his shoes; then he cuts out the shape and colors the resulting butterfly wings as desired. Next he fashions a butterfly body and head from construction paper. He uses a white crayon to add desired facial features before he glues the cutout(s) near the center of the wings. To finish his fancy flier, he attaches bent pipe-cleaner antennae.

Kara Main
Penn Wood Elementary School
West Chester, PA

Ladybug, Ladybug

When it comes to showcasing students' writing, this unique idea is sure to hit the spot! On a 4" x 6" index card, ask each student to pen a poem about ladybugs or respond to a prompt on this topic. Have her use the materials and directions below to make a ladybug. Then instruct her to open its wings and glue her writing inside!

Materials for one ladybug:

9" paper plate	paintbrush
9" red construction paper circle (body)	brad
4" black construction paper circle (head)	hole puncher
black construction paper scraps	scissors
red and black tempera paint	glue

Steps:

1. Paint the back of the paper plate red. Allow it to dry. Paint on black spots.
2. Glue the black circle head onto the red circle body as shown.
3. Cut two antennae from the black construction paper scraps. Glue them in place.
4. Flip the prepared circles.
5. Cut the paper plate in half to make wings. Hole-punch the top of each wing.
6. Use a brad to fasten the wings to the top of the body.

Meghan J. Cuddeback
Albion Primary School
Albion, NY

Step 2

Little Ladybugs

Count on students to go buggy over these handy garden visitors! To begin, glue a three-inch black semicircle (head) to a five-inch black construction paper circle (body) to resemble a ladybug. Cut two antennae from construction paper scraps and glue them on. Turn the ladybug over. Next, fold a 9" x 12" sheet of red construction paper in half to 6" x 9". With fingers either outstretched or together, trace one hand on the folded paper. Carefully cut along the tracing through both thicknesses of the paper. Then position the hand cutouts on the ladybug to resemble wings. Glue them in place. Use black tempera paint to make thumbprints on the wings. Allow the paint to dry; then the spotted critter will be ready for display!

Carol Hargett
Fairborn, OH

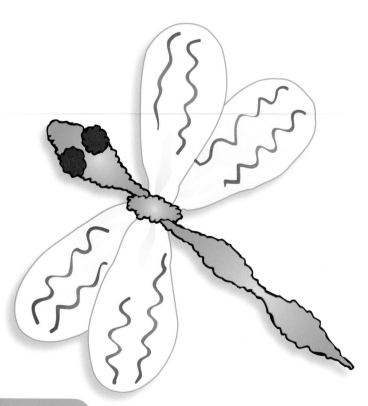

Dazzling Dragonfly

Sporting delicate wings like its real-life counterpart, this dragonfly impostor is made to dazzle. Snip one pointed end from a 12-inch chenille bump pipe cleaner. About one-half inch from the cut end, glue two small pom-pom eyes. To make the wings, draw dark, wavy crayon lines on each of two 3" x 12" strips of waxed paper. Round the corners and pinch the middle of each strip. Wrap the prepared pipe cleaner around the wings.

Darcy Brown
Elon College Elementary
Elon College, NC

Friendly Fireflies

Students' faces are sure to light up when they make these adorable firefly note holders!

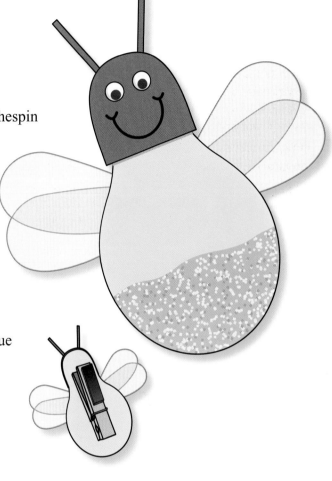

Materials for one note holder:

2 yellow firefly body cutouts   scissors
   (patterns on page 107)   glue
brown construction paper scraps   tape
1" x 5" waxed paper strips   paintbrush
black marker   spring-type clothespin
2 small wiggle eyes   magnetic tape
gold glitter

Steps:

1. Glue a slightly larger piece of brown paper onto the narrow end of one body cutout. Trim the paper to resemble a firefly head.
2. Round the ends of the waxed paper strips. Stack the strips and then pinch them in the middle. Tape them to the back of the prepared body. Gently fan out the resulting wings.
3. Cut two antennae from brown construction paper. Glue them to the back of the head.
4. Glue the undecorated body cutout to the back of the prepared body.
5. On the front of the project, glue two eyes and draw a mouth.
6. Use a paintbrush to spread glue on the lower part of the body. Sprinkle on glitter and then shake off the excess.
7. After the glue dries, glue a clothespin to the back of the firefly and adhere a strip of magnetic tape to it as shown.

Carol Hargett
Fairborn, OH

Sunny Plaque

To make a plaque, begin by preparing a number of triangle cutouts. Glue the cutouts along the edge of a cardboard circle so that they point outward and extend beyond it. To decorate the inner portion of the plaque, prepare additional sets of construction paper cutouts in various shapes. Working from the outer edge of the plaque toward the center, glue each set of shapes in concentric rings to make a design with an open center. If desired, glue on folded cutouts to create a three-dimensional effect. Fashion facial features from construction paper scraps and glue them in the center. Then use masking tape to secure a narrow ribbon hanger to the back of the project.

Amy Barsanti
Nags Head, NC

Magnetic Picture Frame

These handcrafted picture frames will attract plenty of attention from fathers and other chosen recipients. Securely mount a photo on colorful poster board. Trim the poster board as needed to leave a 1½- to 2-inch margin on all sides. To decorate the resulting frame, use a fine-tip marker or a glitter pen to write, "[Name], I've 'bean' wanting to tell you how much I love you!" Then use glue and dried beans in a variety of colors to add other decorations. Lastly, attach a strip of magnetic tape to the back of the project that is just slightly shorter than the width of the frame. Someone is going to be very excited to exhibit this gift of love!

D. Martinez
Fredericksburg Christian School
Fredericksburg, VA

Dad, I've "bean" wanting to tell you how much I love you!

Fancy Pencil Holder

This gift is perfect for Dad or another special person.

Materials for one pencil holder:

clean, empty 12 oz. juice can
$4\frac{1}{2}$" x 9" rectangle of Con-Tact paper
   (for shirt)
fine-tip permanent marker
two $\frac{5}{8}$" x 9" lengths of craft ribbon
   (for tie)
decorative button (for tie tack)
two small buttons (for shirt)
tape
scissors
craft glue
pencils

Steps:

1. Use the marker to write a personalized message in the center of the Con-Tact paper.
2. Peel the backing from the paper. Adhere the paper to the can, making sure the message is legible when the can is upright (opening at the top).
3. To make the tie, tape the ends of one ribbon length to a tabletop and loop the second ribbon length under the ribbon as shown in diagram A. Refer to the remaining diagrams to tie a necktie-type knot. (For best results, have parent volunteers provide assistance with this step.)
4. Remove the tape from the ribbon ends. Glue one ribbon end near the top rim of the can, above the written message. Wrap the ribbon around the can, overlap the ribbon ends, and glue.
5. Position the resulting tie over the paper seam at the front of the can. Trim and shape the ends of the tie as desired.
6. Glue the tie where the decorative button (tie tack) will be attached.
7. Glue the tie tack and small buttons in place as shown.
8. Place the pencils in the resulting holder.

Jane Manuel
Wellington, TX

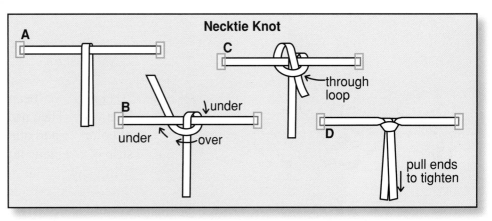

Coastline Beacons

Have students create these models at the conclusion of a lighthouse-related book.

Materials for one lighthouse model:

9" foam plate
three 16 oz. foam cups
two 4" black poster board circles
1" x 8" yellow construction paper strip
small amount of sand
decorations such as Spanish moss and small
  seashells, pinecones, or stones

tempera paint
paintbrush
black marker
masking tape
scissors
stapler
glue

Step 7

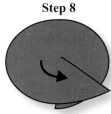

Step 8

Steps:

1. Turn the plate upside down and spread glue on it. Sprinkle sand onto the glue. Gently shake off any excess.
2. Glue the cups together to make a stack. Allow the glue to dry.
3. Turn the stack of cups upside down and then paint it to resemble a lighthouse.
4. Glue the lighthouse and decorations onto the plate.
5. Glue one poster board circle atop the lighthouse.
6. Draw window panes on the yellow strip. Staple the ends to make a circle.
7. Place the circle on the poster board circle glued to the lighthouse. Tape it into place as shown.
8. Make a cut in the second poster board circle from the edge to the center. Form a cone (see the illustration). Staple the overlapping poster board.
9. Squeeze glue along the top of the yellow circle. Gently set the cone in place.

Claudine Swan
Wright Elementary School
Altoona, PA

Telling T-Shirts

Create a fashion statement with student-designed T-shirts!

Materials for one self-likeness:
white construction paper copy of page 108
9" x 12" sheet of skin-toned construction
    paper
9" x 12" sheet of construction paper (pants)
3" x 12" strip of construction paper (shoes)
5½" circle template
construction paper scraps for hair
crayons or markers
scissors
glue
clear tape

Step 4

Steps:

1. Illustrate the T-shirt (pattern on page 108) to reveal your personal interests.
2. Trace the circle template on the skin-toned paper. Cut out the resulting shape. Add construction paper hair, facial features, and other desired details to create a likeness of yourself.
3. Cut arms and a neck from the remaining skin-toned paper.
4. To make the pants, fold the remaining sheet of construction paper in half (to 4½" x 12") and trim it (see illustration). Unfold and decorate the pants.
5. To make the shoes, fold the paper strip in half (to 3" x 6") and cut a shoe shape from the folded paper. Decorate the shoes.
6. Assemble the project as shown.

Joyce A. Chestney
Baker Elementary
Altoona, PA

Three-Dimensional Art

To make a three-dimensional project, fold a 12-inch square of white construction paper in half diagonally and then fold the folded paper in half. Unfold the paper and position it so the fold lines form a *t*. Draw and color your school on the top half of the paper, making sure the school sits on the fold line. Next, cut the bottom half of the paper in half, using the fold line as a guide. Overlap the two pieces to form the bottom of the project. Use a pencil to lightly sketch a sidewalk leading away from the school. Then lay the project flat and color the sidewalk and desired landscaping. Reassemble the project and glue the overlapping pieces. On a 4" x 5" piece of white construction paper, illustrate yourself. Cut out the picture, leaving a tab (for gluing) at the bottom. Fold back the tab and glue it on the sidewalk.

Jo Fryer
Kildeer Countryside School
Long Grove, IL

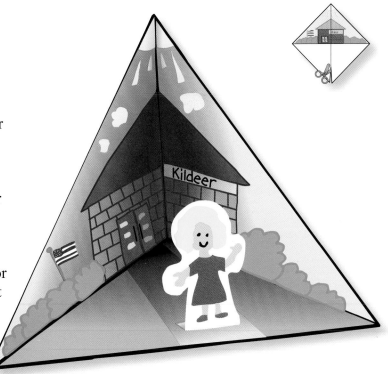

Me Monuments

With a pinch here and a pat there, students can create monuments spotlighting themselves. Give each child a sheet of waxed paper and two golf ball–sized portions of Crayola Model Magic modeling compound. Or prepare your favorite paintable, air-drying dough recipe. Working atop his waxed paper, a child forms a shape from one ball of dough that represents a favorite interest or hobby. With the remaining ball of dough, he forms a base for his shape. Then he molds the shape to the base. When his resulting monument is dry, he paints it as desired.

Kathy Moore
Stone Creek Elementary School
Rockford, IL

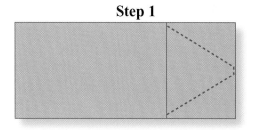

Step 1

Crayon Buddy

Create a colorful display of student-made crayon buddies!

Materials for one crayon buddy:
6" x 9" construction paper rectangle (for crayon)
two 4½" x 6" construction paper rectangles (for crayon tip, hands, and feet)
two ¾" x 6" black construction paper strips
four 1" x 9" black construction paper strips
pencil
glue
black marker
scissors
stapler

Steps:
1. Position one small rectangle horizontally. Draw a crayon tip on it as illustrated and then cut it out.
2. Glue the large rectangle to the tip to resemble a crayon.
3. Make a thin, wavy cut along the long sides of each short black strip. Then glue the strips onto the crayon as shown.
4. Use the marker to draw a face.
5. Accordion-fold the long black strips. Staple them in place to make two arms and two legs.
6. Fold the remaining rectangle in half and then in half again. Unfold it and then cut the rectangle into quarters.
7. Cut an oval from each quarter to make hands and feet. Glue them in place.

Sheila Criqui-Kelley
Lebo Elementary
Lebo, KS

Going Dotty!

Have students practice pointillism with this pleasing display idea! To make a painting, a student lightly sketches a simple figure on a six-inch square of white paper. For easy handling while he paints, the youngster uses two pieces of tape to secure the top and bottom of his paper to his work surface. Then he dips a cotton swab into a desired color of tempera paint. He presses it repeatedly on his paper, making dots close together to fill in a desired portion of his figure. He reloads the cotton swab with paint as needed. Using a different cotton swab for each color of paint, he repeats this process until his entire figure is painted. After the paint dries, he mounts his artwork on a seven-inch construction paper square.

Arrange students' artwork in a row along a classroom wall. Point out to students how the dots of paint seem to blend together when their artwork is viewed from a distance.

Dazzling Dots

Add an outdoor touch to a simple work of art. Draw a large desired object on white construction paper. Then head outdoors with the drawing and crayons. Place the drawing faceup on a dry sidewalk. Carefully color the drawing, bearing down hard while coloring. (The object will look as if it were colored with tiny dots.) Then return to the classroom and create a backdrop for the object by coloring the rest of the paper on a smooth surface. Mount the completed project on a slightly larger sheet of brightly colored construction paper.

Elizabeth Searls Almy
Greensboro, NC

Impressive Projects

This nifty fingerpainting idea has striking results and no messy cleanup! To begin, draw a simple scribble design with heavy crayon lines on a 9" x 12" sheet of white paper. Use brightly colored crayons to color in the design. Next, place the paper on a newspaper-covered surface and put on a pair of disposable rubber gloves. Squeeze a puddle of liquid tempera paint onto the paper. Mix in a few drops of liquid starch. Spread the mixture over the entire sheet of paper (add more paint if needed). Then use your fingers to make a desired design. After the paint dries, staple the artwork to a larger sheet of construction paper to frame it.

Janette E. Anderson
Fremont, CA

Plastic Wrap Paintings

Anything goes with this hands-on approach to painting! Use tape to secure the top and bottom edges of a 9" x 12" sheet of art paper to a section of newspaper. Randomly drip colorful tempera paint onto the art paper and then cover the art paper with plastic wrap. Touching only the plastic, use your hands to smooth, smear, and swirl the paint colors. When a desired effect is achieved, remove the plastic and allow drying time. Next, peel away the tape and trim the painting into a desired shape. Mount the shape onto a complementary color of construction paper and then trim the paper to create an eye-catching border.

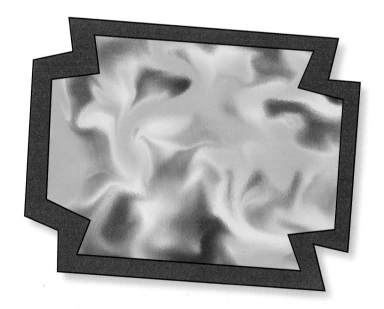

Abstract Artwork

Encourage oodles of creativity with this impressive project. Use a pencil to make several dots on an 8" x 10" sheet of white paper; then use a ruler and colorful markers or crayons to connect the dots. To make a frame for the design, center a 7" x 8" template atop a 9" x 12" sheet of colorful construction paper. Trace around the template; then draw two intersecting diagonal lines in the resulting rectangle. Carefully cut along the diagonal lines and fold back the flaps along the remaining lines. Tape the design to the back of the frame so the artwork is viewed through the opening and then decorate the frame as desired. Each piece of abstract artwork will be unique!

Rita Arnold
Alden Hebron School
Hebron, IL

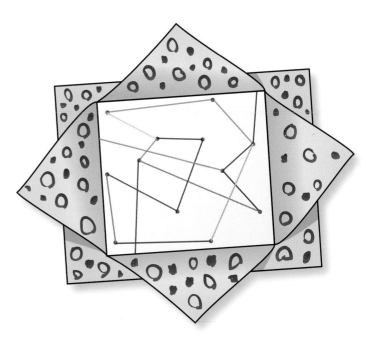

Pretty Patchwork

Brighten your classroom with a unique patchwork display! To make a quilt square, a student cuts patches of a chosen color from discarded magazines and catalogs. Then he places a seven-inch white construction paper square on a slightly larger piece of waxed paper. He glues the color patches onto the square, overlapping the patches and extending them slightly beyond the square to ensure that the square is completely covered. After the glue is dry, he trims the excess. Then he mounts the decorated square onto a nine-inch construction paper square in a contrasting color. Arrange students' completed patchwork projects on a wall to create an eye-catching (and colorful!) quilt.

adapted from an idea by Amy Barsanti
Nags Head, NC

Twist, Curl, and Bend!

Spark students' imaginations with this three-dimensional art project. In advance, prepare a supply of 1" x 9" construction paper strips in a variety of colors. To make a project, a student places a 9" x 12" sheet of tagboard on a work surface. If desired, he cuts chosen strips into shorter lengths. He manipulates several strips in a variety of ways, such as folding, bending, twisting, and curling (by wrapping them around a pencil). Then he glues them onto the tagboard to create a three-dimensional effect.

adapted from an idea by Heather Miller
Auburn, IN

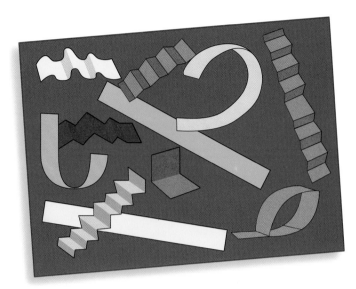

Lacy Artwork

This project uses layers of cut paper to create an eye-catching effect.

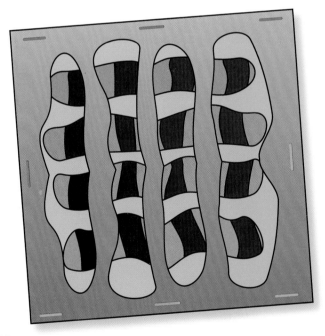

Materials for one project:
9" square of black construction paper
three 9" squares of paper in different colors
scissors
stapler

Steps:
1. Set the black paper aside. Fold one square of colored paper in half.
2. Cutting from the fold toward the opposite edge, cut out a narrow, irregular shape, taking care not to cut all the way to the edge. Cut out several additional shapes. (See the illustration.)
3. Unfold the paper and put it aside.
4. Repeat Steps 2 and 3 with the remaining colorful squares.
5. Stack the prepared squares atop the black square. Turn the colorful squares and rearrange the order of them until a desired effect is achieved.
6. Align the squares and then staple them together along the outer edges.

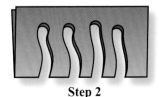

Step 2

Joan M. Macey
Binghamton, NY

Colorful Spacecraft

Looking for an out-of-this-world art experience? Try this! Use crayons or markers to decorate the back of two white, dessert-size paper plates. From the rim of one plate, cut a semicircle opening. Then glue or tape the plate rims together, keeping the artwork to the outside. To create an alien look-alike, cut two antennae shapes from the paper plate scrap. Glue a wiggle eye to one end of each shape and glue the other end of each shape to the same large pom-pom. When the glue is dry, glue the pom-pom alien inside the spacecraft opening. Before these colorful space-crafts and their alien passengers blast off to another universe, ask students to write and illustrate far-out tales about their newfound friends.

Faye Fowler Haney
Valley View Elementary
Jonesboro, AR

Somewhere in Space

To begin this painting project, a student uses red, orange, and yellow crayons to completely cover a sheet of white construction paper with patches of color. Then he prepares a desired number of tagboard stars and circles (planets). He tacks each cutout to his paper with a loop of tape. Next, he uses black tempera paint and a sponge to paint his entire paper. While the paint is wet, he sprinkles on silver glitter. After the paint dries, he carefully removes the cutouts and shakes off any excess glitter.

Tara Hartline
Allatoona Elementary
Acworth, GA

Marvelous Moon

To make a moon-themed painting, a student places a seven-inch white paper circle on a newspaper-covered surface. She cuts provided coarse sandpaper into assorted shapes and then glues the shapes onto the circle. Then she sponge-paints the circle with gray tempera paint. After the paint dries, she glues the circle onto a 9" x 12" sheet of black construction paper. She dips the end of a paintbrush into white paint and then presses it repeatedly on the black paper to make stars. She repeats this process until she achieves a desired effect.

Elizabeth Searls Almy
Greensboro, NC

Wild Thing Puppet

Spark imaginations with this monstrously fun follow-up to Maurice Sendak's *Where the Wild Things Are.*

Materials for one puppet:

1½ paper plates
two 2" x 4" gray construction paper rectangles
two 2" yellow construction paper squares
2½" construction paper square (Colors may vary.)
2" x 9" construction paper rectangle (Colors may vary.)
several dried lima beans

crayons
scissors
glue
stapler

Steps:

1. Cut a circle from each yellow paper square to make two eyes. Use crayons to add pupils. Glue the eyes to the rounded side of the whole paper plate.
2. Cut a nose from the 2½-inch construction paper square. Glue it in place.
3. Draw a mouth. Glue on lima beans for teeth.
4. Cut two horns from the gray construction paper rectangles. Staple them to the back of the plate.
5. Tear or cut the 2" x 9" construction paper rectangle into strips to make hair. Glue the strips in place.
6. Staple the paper plate half to the back of the project as shown.

Step 6

adapted from an idea by Elizabeth Searls Almy

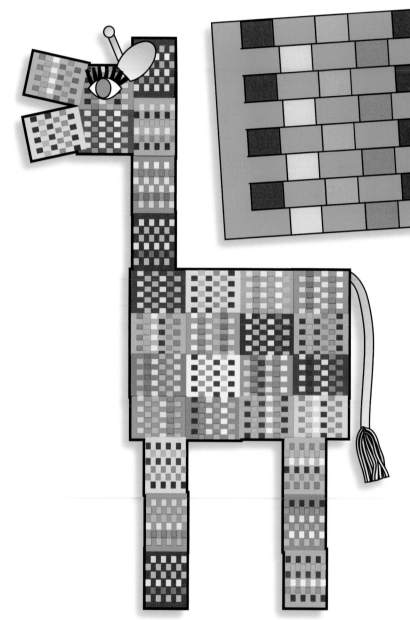

Woven Giraffe

There's more to this weaving project than meets the eye! To make a rectangular weaving, fold a 9" x 12" sheet of colorful construction paper in half (to 6" x 9"). Starting at the fold, cut a series of one-inch strips, stopping approximately one inch from the open ends. Unfold the resulting loom and weave six 1½" x 9" colorful construction paper strips in the loom. Glue the ends of each woven strip in place. Assemble the completed projects into a giraffe shape like the one shown. Invite students to study the colorful critter and submit proposals for other critters to be woven. Then let the weaving continue!

Lisa Strieker
St. Paul Elementary
Highland, IL

Cutie-Pie Cowpoke

Saddle up for this rootin'-tootin' art project! You just may lasso some of your buckaroos' geometry skills too!

Materials for one cowpoke:
two 6" squares of light blue construction paper (pants)
one 6" square of dark blue construction paper (shirt)
one 3" square of red construction paper (bandana)
one 3" circle of skin-toned construction paper (head)
brown construction paper copy of the hat, boot,
    and glove patterns on page 109
construction paper scraps
markers or crayons
scissors
glue

Steps:

1. Cut out the hat, boot, and glove patterns. Set them aside.

2. To make the body, fold each of the three six-inch squares in half to create a triangle. Position the dark blue triangle (shirt) with the fold at the top Unfold the paper and glue each glove cutout directly below the crease line. Next glue the two light blue triangles in place to create pants; then refold the shirt and glue it closed.

3. Glue each boot cutout to the bottom of a pant leg.

4. To make the bandana, fold the red construction paper square in half to create a triangle; then slide the top of the shirt inside the resulting bandana and glue the bandana in place.

5. Glue the hat cutout to the top of the skin-toned circle. Use markers or crayons to add facial features to the circle; then glue the resulting head to the top of the bandana.

6. Use the construction paper scraps and markers to decorate your cowpoke.

Kim Clemente
Schnieder Grade School
Farmer City, IL

Shapely Critters

Encourage students to let their imaginations run wild as they consider animal subjects for this art project! To begin, share Lois Ehlert's *Color Farm* or *Color Zoo* with your students. Prompt plenty of discussion about the shapes that Lois Ehlert uses and the effects that she achieves. To make a shapely critter, a student cuts out different-sized paper circles, triangles, and rectangles in a variety of colors. Next she manipulates the cutouts on paper of a contrasting color. When the student has created an eye-catching animal likeness, she glues the cutouts in place.

Valerie Smith
Exton, PA

Pizza With Pizzazz

Tempt your youngsters' tastebuds with this multisensory pizza project! To make a pizza, lightly color the rim of a six-inch paper plate brown. Make desired construction paper toppings and then set them aside. Mix red food coloring into white glue so that it resembles the color of tomato sauce. Brush the glue mixture onto the uncolored portion of the paper plate. While the project is wet, sprinkle oregano on top and press the toppings in place.

For a mouthwatering follow-up, have each student respond to a pizza-related writing prompt. Display each student's writing and completed pizza on a bulletin board titled "Pizza! Pizza!"

Jodi Bodenheimer
Vegas Verdes Elementary
Las Vegas, NV

Terrific Turtles

Students will take a shine to these irresistible reptiles! To make the shell, cut one-inch lengths of masking tape and attach them in an overlapping fashion to an inverted seven-inch paper plate. Be sure to cover the entire plate surface, including the rim. Next use the sponge-tip applicator on a bottle of brown shoe polish to paint the tape-covered plate. When the resulting shell is dry, cut out a turtle head, a tail, and four legs from construction paper. Add desired details to the cutouts with markers and then glue the cutouts under the rim of the painted shell.

Melanie J. Miller
Nashport, OH

Scissors on the Scene

Spark creativity with scissors—no cutting required! To begin, place a pair of scissors on a sheet of drawing paper. Imagine how the outline of the scissors might be incorporated into a scene. Experiment with positioning the scissors both open and closed and on different parts of the paper. When you picture a scene and are satisfied with the placement of the scissors, trace them with a pencil. Set the scissors aside and then use a black marker to retrace the outline. Use crayons or colored pencils to complete the scissors figure. Then complete the scene with background details. Mount the scene on a slightly larger piece of construction paper to frame it. Now that's a simple idea that's a cut above the rest!

Janette E. Anderson
Fremont, CA

Venus Flytrap

Incorporate this snappy project into a plant unit!

Materials for one project:

two 4" circles of green construction paper
two 4" circles of red construction paper
3" x 12" piece of green construction paper
4" x 7" piece of construction paper (Colors may vary.)
9" x 12" sheet of construction paper (Colors may vary.)
1" square of black tissue paper

flat wooden toothpicks
small white coffee filter
glue
scissors
crayons
clear tape

Steps:

1. Fold the four paper circles in half and then unfold each one.
2. Glue toothpicks around the edge of each green circle.
3. Glue a red circle atop each green circle, matching up the fold lines. Fold each resulting trap in half (keeping the red paper to the inside) and then set it aside to dry.
4. Trim the 4" x 7" paper to resemble a planter. Add desired decorations.
5. Cut one long stem and two shorter stems from the green paper.
6. Position the long stem between the shorter stems. Glue the stems and the planter on the 9" x 12" construction paper.
7. Glue a trap to the top of each short stem. Wad up the black tissue paper square and glue it inside one trap.
8. Fold the coffee filter in half and then fold it in half again. Trim one inch from the open end. To form a flower, pinch the point and scrunch the sides of the filter. Tape the point to the top of the long stem. Gently open the blossom and glue the bottom edge of the bloom to the construction paper.

adapted from an idea by Stacy Confer
Jefferson Elementary
Emmaus, PA

Step 3

Bloomin' Bookmarks

Reading skills are sure to blossom with these colorful bookmarks! To begin, make four green leaf cutouts. Make two tulip bloom cutouts (patterns on page 105) from colorful magazine paper. Also cut two 3" x 9" rectangles from clear Con-Tact covering. Peel the backing from one rectangle. Arrange two leaves, one tulip bloom (facedown), and a ½" x 6" green paper stem on the adhesive. Next, carefully glue the remaining leaves and bloom (faceup) atop their like shapes. Then peel the backing from the second rectangle and align the rectangle, adhesive side down, atop the project. Trim the edges of the resulting bookmark, leaving space at the top to punch a hole and add a loop of yarn.

Elizabeth Almy
Greensboro, NC

Fabulous Foam Frame

In addition to being fun to make, this one-of-a-kind photo frame makes a precious gift! To make a frame, cut a piece of colorful craft foam that is slightly larger than the photo itself. For a vertical mount, use a pencil to trace along the top and bottom edges of the photo. For a horizontal mount, trace along the left and right edges. Then remove the picture and use scissors to cut a line that is parallel to and about a half inch inside each pencil line. (See the diagram.) Turn the foam over and insert the photo into the resulting frame. Use glue, scissors, a hole puncher, and colorful scraps of craft foam to add desired decorations. Attach two strips of magnetic tape to the back of the project—one at the top and one at the bottom.

Gina Reagan
Summerfield Elementary
Summerfield, NC

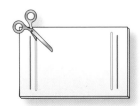

Star-Spangled Sparklers

These festive sparklers are the perfect addition to a patriotic celebration! Glue two red, two white, and two blue 2" x 6" construction paper strips to a large cardboard tube, alternating the colors as shown. Next tape half-inch silver paper strips (cut from wrapping paper) to the inside rim of one end of the tube. Embellish the tube with star-shaped cutouts or foil stickers.

Melissa A. Stanek
Better Beginnings
Oneonta, NY

Red, White, and Blue

Get to the heart of your students' patriotism and creativity! Provide an assortment of red, white, and blue craft supplies, such as construction paper, curling ribbon, pom-poms, and star stickers. Begin by cutting a heart shape from construction paper. Then use the provided supplies to decorate the cutout in a patriotic way. As students work, invite them to explain why they feel proud to live in their country. If desired, write the students' thoughts on a length of bulletin board paper titled "We Love Our Country!" Then display the list and use the students' artwork to create a star-spangled border around it.

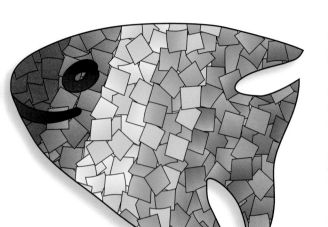

Rainbow Swimmers

Make a colorful splash with these fancy fish! Begin the project with a white construction paper copy of the fish pattern on page 110 and a supply of tissue paper squares in the following rainbow colors: red, orange, yellow, green, blue, and purple. Cut out the fish pattern and then glue the appropriate color of tissue paper squares in each section, overlapping the squares as you go, until the cutout is completely covered. (If desired, use diluted glue and a paintbrush to adhere the tissue paper squares.) After the glue dries, trim excess tissue paper from the edges of the cutout and then use a black marker to draw desired details on the fish.

Gina Marinelli
Bernice Young Elementary School
Burlington, NJ

Waterless Aquarium

This unique aquarium gives a clear view of what's under the sea!

Materials for one aquarium:

two 9-inch white paper plates
piece of blue plastic wrap that is slightly larger than a paper plate
small amount of green shredded paper
construction paper scraps (for fish)
small amount of sand

glue
crayons
scissors
clear tape
access to a stapler

Steps:

1. Squeeze glue onto the lower portion of one paper plate. Sprinkle sand onto the glue. Shake off the excess.
2. Glue on lengths of shredded paper to resemble sea grass.
3. Cut out several fish shapes from construction paper. Add desired crayon details.
4. Glue the fish onto the prepared plate. Allow the glue to dry.
5. Place the prepared plate facedown on the plastic wrap. Tape the plastic wrap to the plate so that it is taut. Then turn the plate faceup.
6. Cut out the inner circle from the undecorated plate to make a ring. Discard the inner portion.
7. Staple the ring to the decorated plate so that the rounded side is facing out.

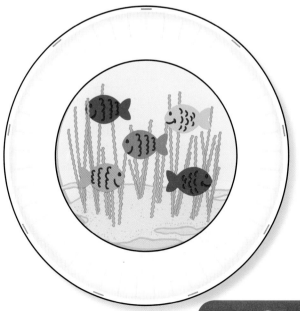

Mary Beth Knippel
Madison, WI

Apple Patterns
Use with "Apple Notecards" on page 6.

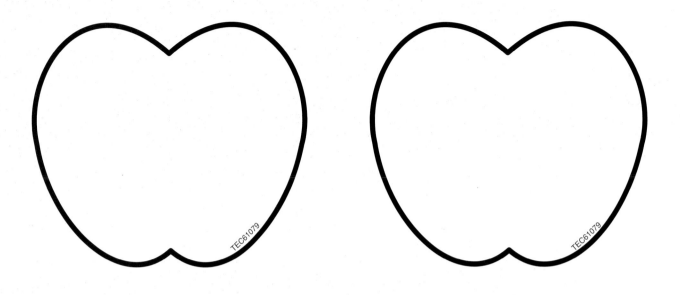

Apple Patterns
Use with "Fancy Apples" on page 8.

TEC61079

Leaf Patterns
Use with "Brightening the Breezes" on page 11.

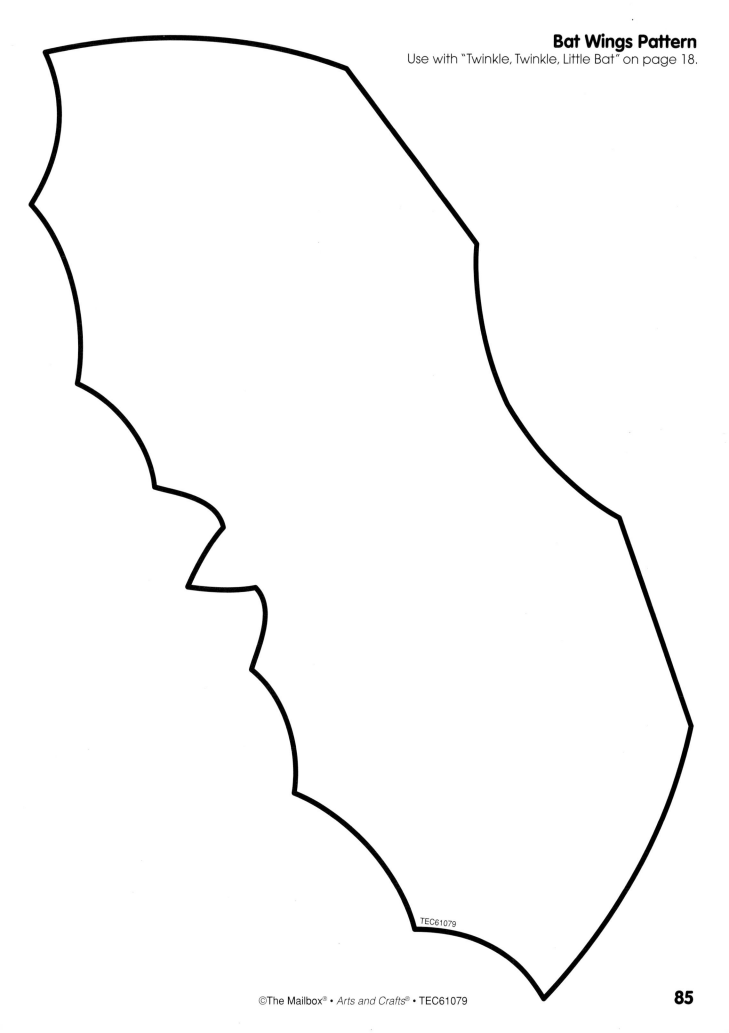

Bat Wings Pattern
Use with "Twinkle, Twinkle, Little Bat" on page 18.

TEC61079

Cat Pattern

Use with "Illuminating Cats" on page 19.

TEC61079

TEC61079

Triangle Pattern
Use with "Star of David" on page 23.

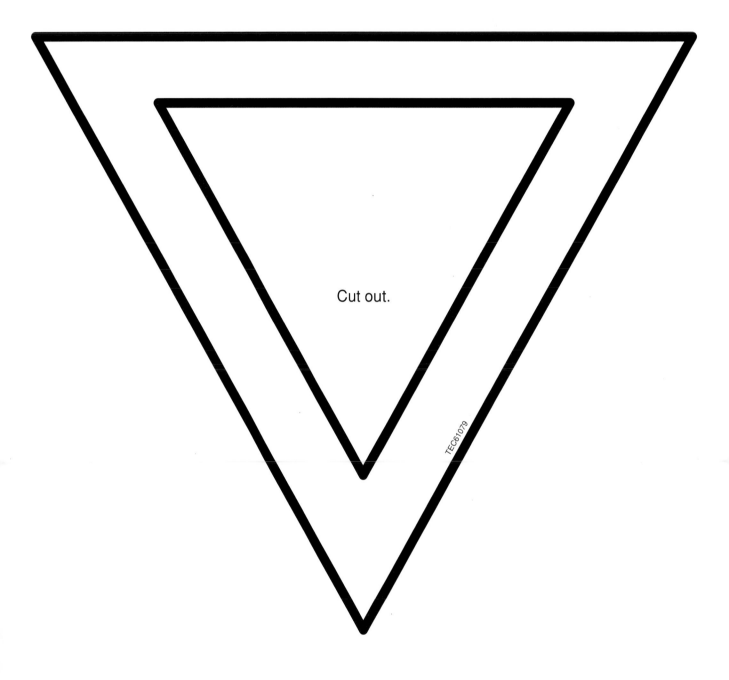

Cut out.

TEC61079

TEC61079

TEC61079

Gingerbread Decorations

Circle each answer that describes you.
Then follow the directions to make decorations for your project.

Which Am I?

girl = pink
boy = blue

Cut out two eyes from the color you circled.

How Old Am I?

6 = orange

7 = red

8 = green

9 or older = yellow

Cut out a nose (△) from the color you circled.

How Many Brothers?

0　1　2　3　4　5　more

For each brother, cut out one white stripe for each arm.

How Many Sisters?

0　1　2　3　4　5　more

For each sister, cut out one white stripe for each leg.

When Is My Birthday?

January	=	white blue
February	=	red pink
March	=	green yellow
April	=	yellow purple
May	=	pink green
June	=	blue green
July	=	red white blue
August	=	yellow red
September	=	blue red
October	=	orange black
November	=	yellow brown
December	=	red green

Cut out hair from the colors you circled.

What Do I Like to Do?

read	=	blue
watch TV	=	white
play outdoors	=	red
play indoors	=	black
use a computer	=	orange
draw pictures	=	purple
write stories	=	green
dance	=	yellow

Make one button for each circled item.

What Pet Do I Like Best?

dog	=
cat	=
fish	=
bird	=
other	=

Draw the mouth that matches your answer.

Note to the teacher: Use with "A Gingerbread Glyph" on page 27.

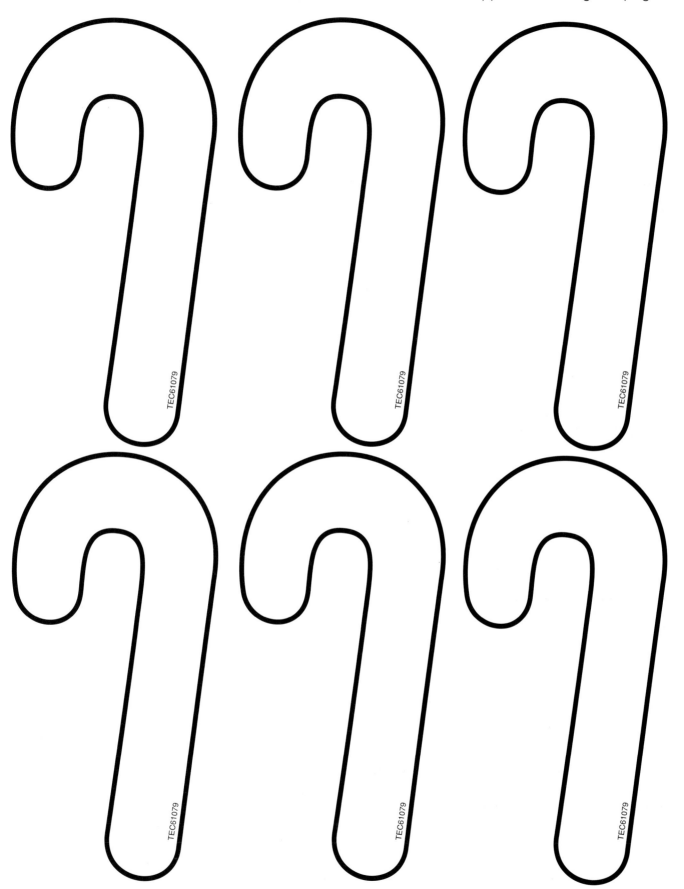

Reindeer Face Pattern

Use with "Irresistible Reindeer" on page 28.

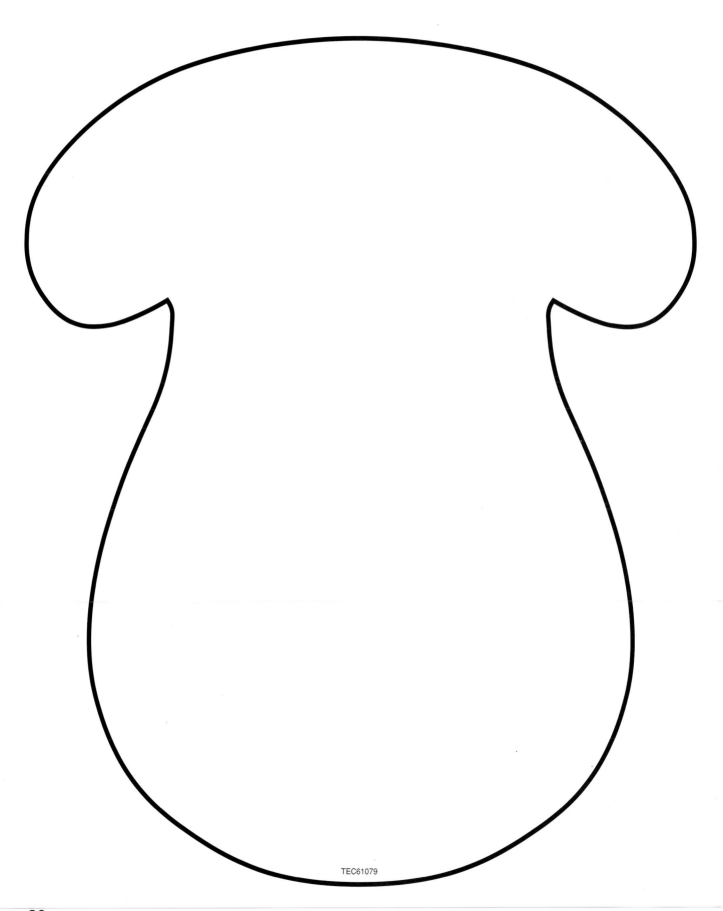

TEC61079

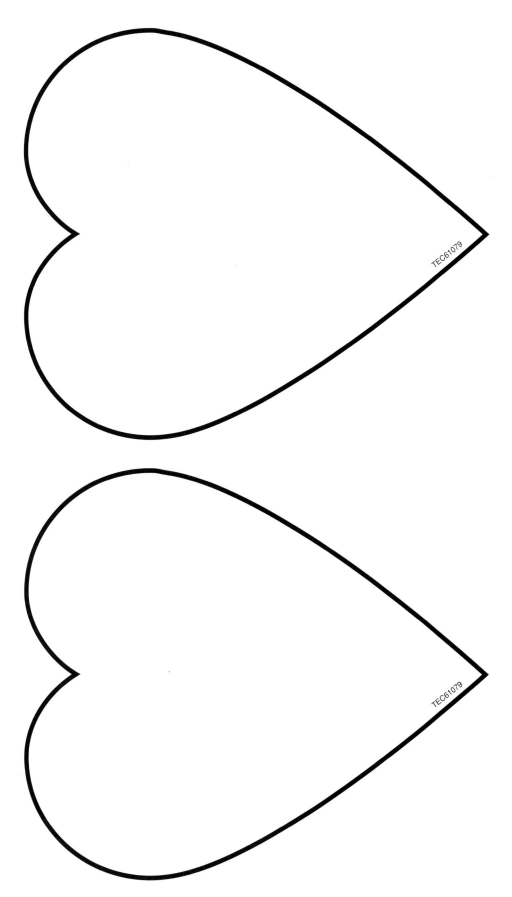

TEC61079

TEC61079

Bell Pattern

Use with "Beautiful Bell" on page 32.

TEC61079

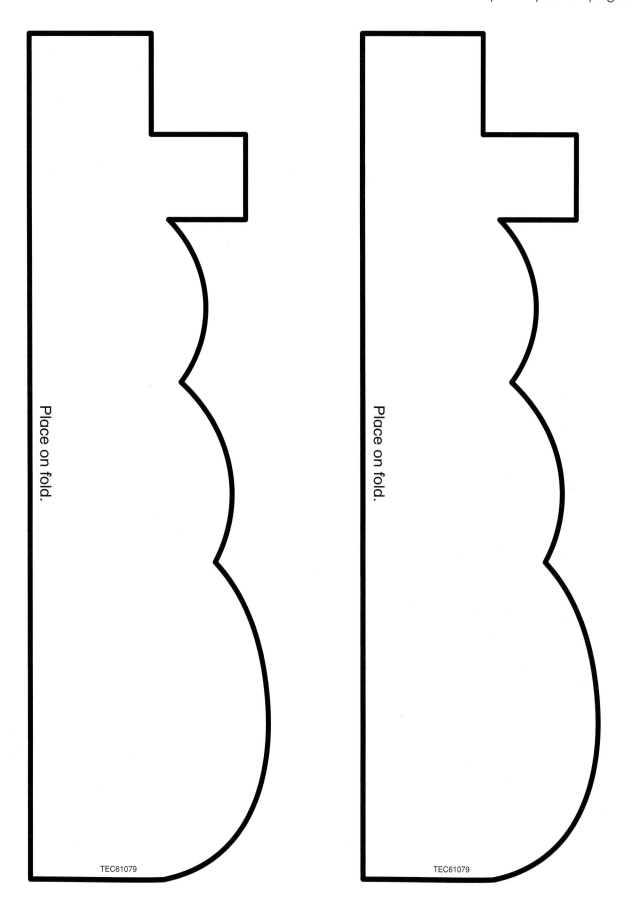

Place on fold.

Place on fold.

TEC61079

TEC61079

Earmuff and Nose Patterns
Use with "Cool Carriers" on page 38.

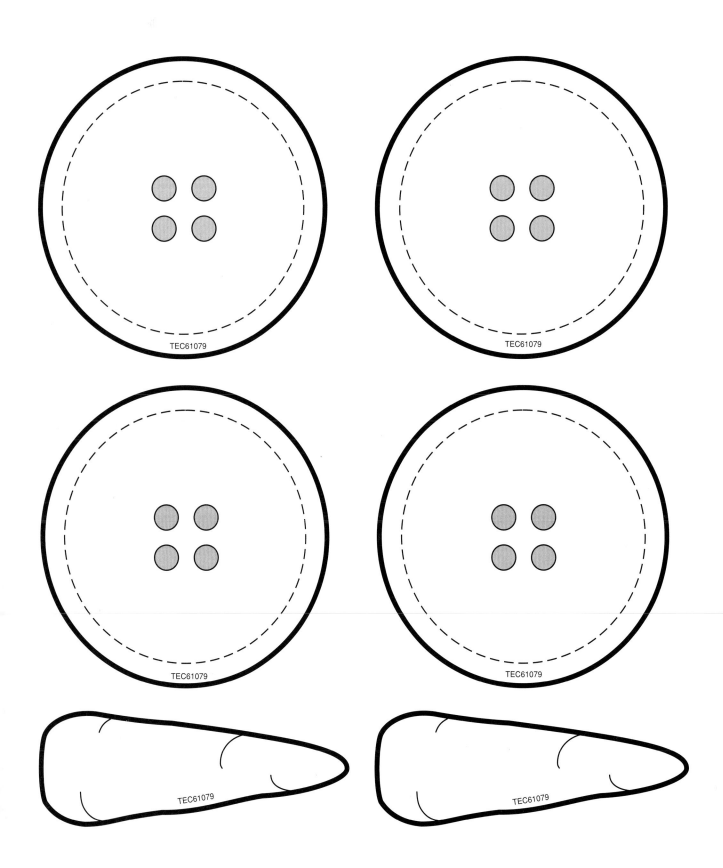

TEC61079

TEC61079

TEC61079

TEC61079

TEC61079

TEC61079

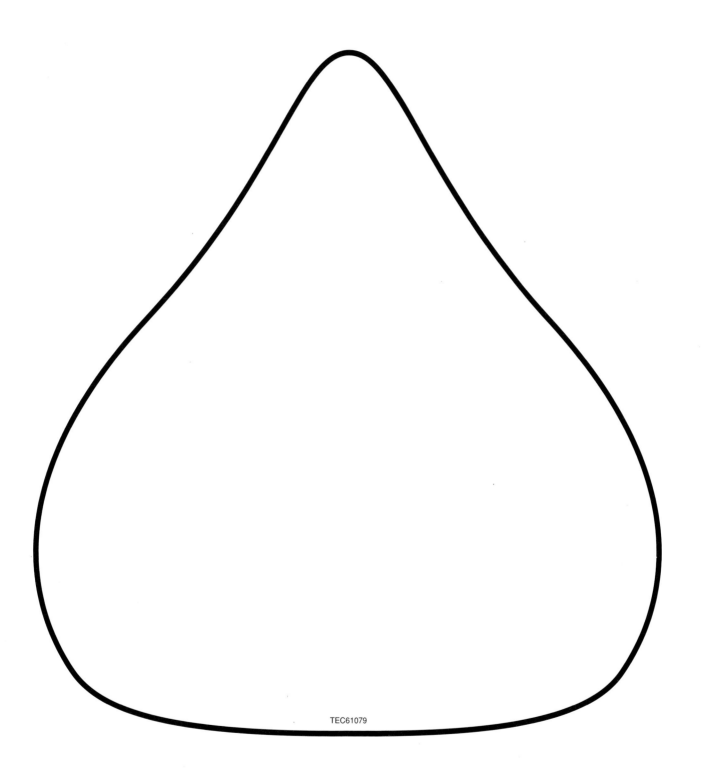

TEC61079

Face and Ear Patterns
Use with "Woolly Lambs" on page 46.

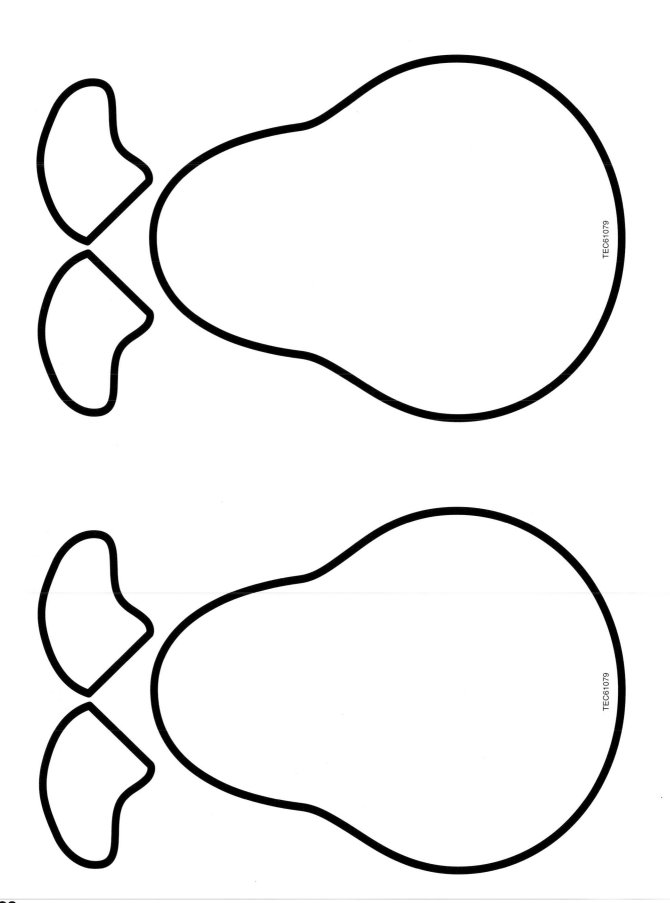

TEC61079

TEC61079

TEC61079

St. Patrick's Day Patterns

Use with "St. Patrick's Day Mobile" on page 49.

TEC61079

TEC61079

TEC61079

Egg Pattern

Use with "Eggs Extraordinaire" and "Pretty Pasta Eggs" on page 50.

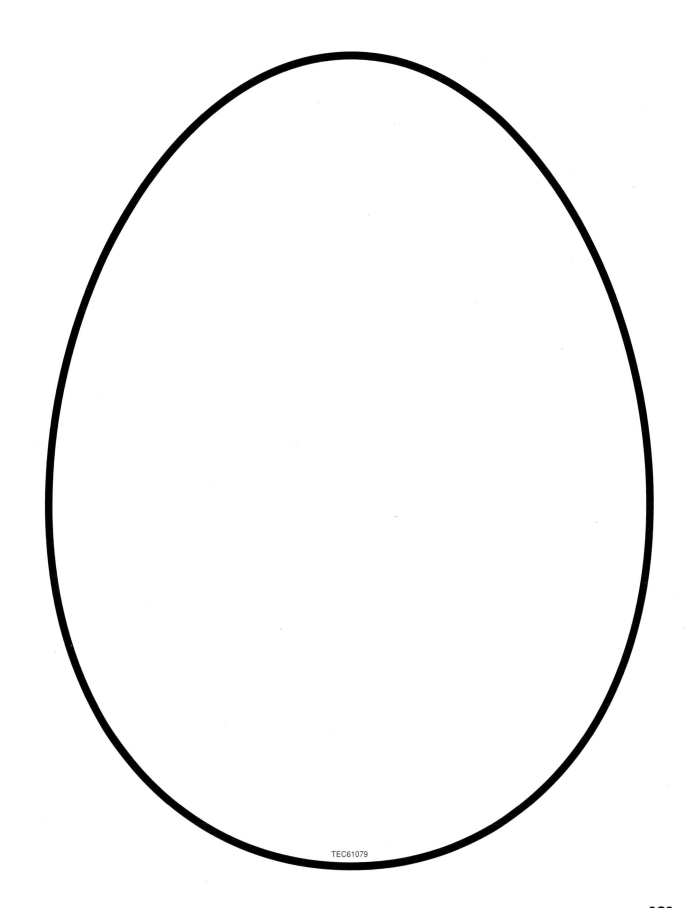

TEC61079

Duck Pattern
Use with "Country Duck" on page 53.

TEC61079

bill

foot

hat

wing

tail

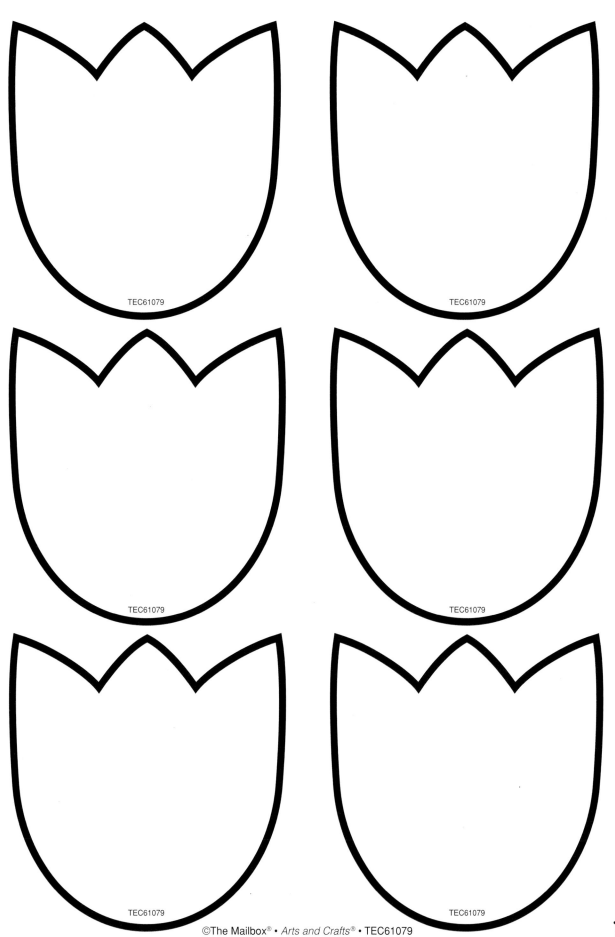

TEC61079

TEC61079

TEC61079

TEC61079

TEC61079

TEC61079

Poem Patterns
Use with "Handmade Butterflies" on page 58.

From my hands a butterfly,

A part of me for you.

I made it just for Mother's Day,

To say that I love you!

TEC61079

From my hands a butterfly,

A part of me for you.

I made it just for Mother's Day,

To say that I love you!

TEC61079

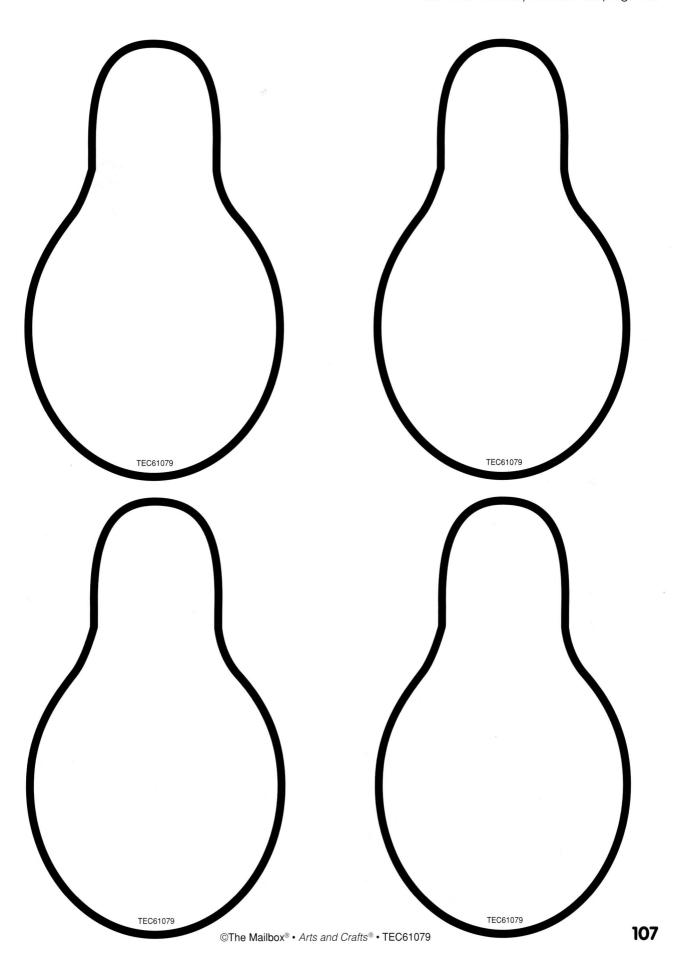

TEC61079

TEC61079

TEC61079

TEC61079

T-Shirt Pattern
Use with "Telling T-Shirts" on page 65.

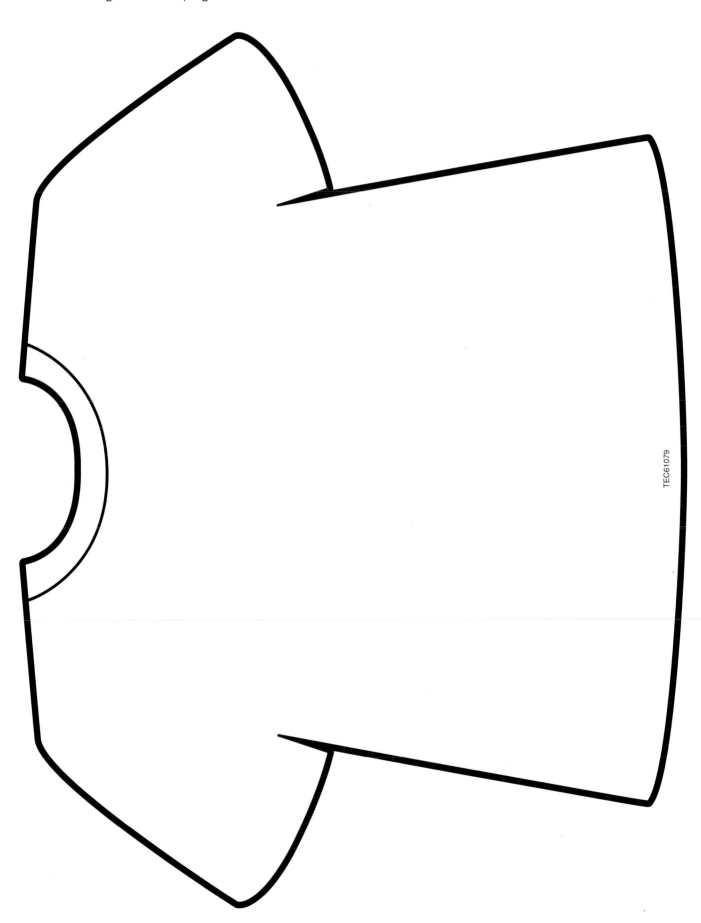

TEC61079

TEC61079

Fish Pattern
Use with "Rainbow Swimmers" on page 81.

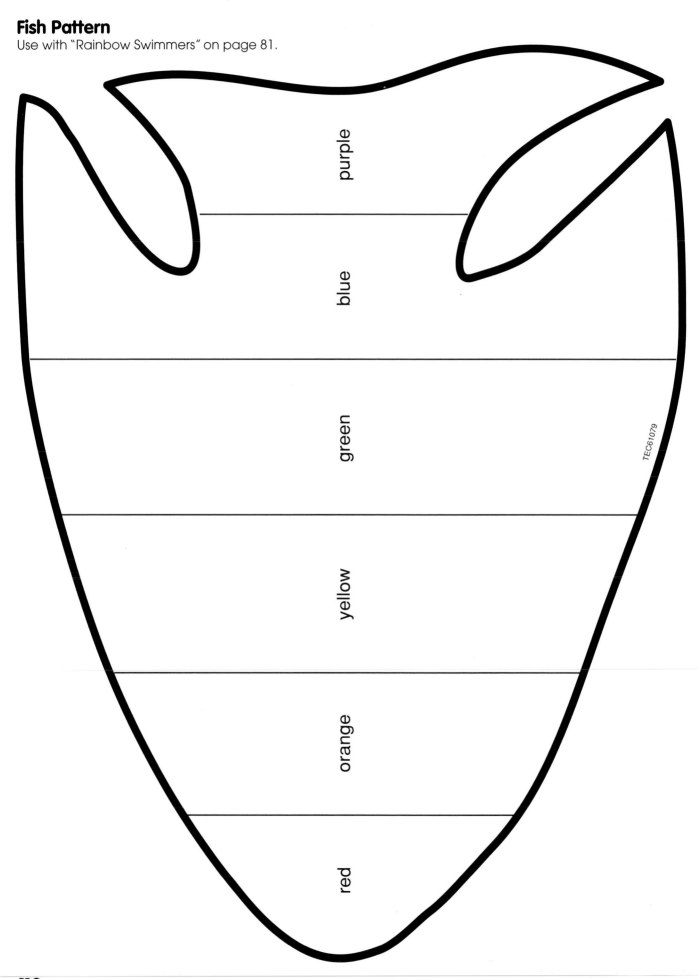

purple

blue

green

yellow

orange

red

TEC61079

Index